Playing with Plays™
Presents

Pumpkins, Potions, and Poe

Where Heads Roll, Minds Split, And Ravens Talk Back

A play in 3 Acts
Creatively modified by
Brendan P. Kelso

Ensemble cast size:
Minimum of 15 actors, up to 57!

Table Of Contents

Copyright 3

Director's Notes 4

Setting the Stage 5

Cast of Characters 6

Introduction 11

The Legend of Sleepy Hollow 13

First Transition 41

The Strange Case of Dr. Jekyll & Mr. Hyde 42

Second Transition 69

Edgar Allan Poe Mashup 71

About the Author 93

Sneak Peek at other full-length and 1-act plays 94

Playing with Plays™ – Pumpkins, Potions, and Poe

Copyright © 2004-2025 by Brendan P. Kelso. All rights reserved. Used with permission by Playing with Plays LLC

No part of this book may be reproduced in any form or by any electronic or mechanical means, including photocopying, recording, information storage or retrieval systems now known or to be invented, without permission in writing from the publisher, except by a reviewer, who may quote brief passages in a review, written for inclusion within a periodical. Any members of education institutions wishing to photocopy part or all of the work for classroom use, or publishers who would like to obtain permission to include the work in an anthology, should send their inquiries to the publisher. We monitor the internet for cases of piracy and copyright infringement/violations. We will pursue all cases within the full extent of the law.

CAUTION: Professionals and amateurs are hereby warned that all plays published by Playing With Plays may be produced only pursuant to a signed written license and are subject to payment of a royalty. The plays are fully protected under the copyright laws of the United States, Canada, the United Kingdom, and all other countries of the Berne Union,. All rights, including dramatic (both amateur and professional), motion picture, radio, television, recitation, public reading, internet, and any method of photographic reproduction are strictly reserved.

Whenever a Playing With Plays play is performed, the following must be included on all programs, printing and advertising for the play: © 2004-2025 by Brendan P. Kelso. All rights reserved. Performed under license from, Playing with Plays LLC, www.PlayingWithPlays.com.

For performance rights please contact:

contact@PlayingWithPlays.com

Please note, for special circumstances, we do waive copyright and performance fees.
Rules subject to change

www.PlayingWithPlays.com

Printed in the United States of America

ISBN: 978-1-954571-34-1

Director's Note

Congratulations! You have been given a rare gift of infusing the incredible classics of amazing gothic, horror, authors into the minds and hearts of your actors and audience. Fun!

I originally wrote Shakespeare for Kids books to open the door for kids to love Shakespeare and his storylines. Over time, and reaching over 100,000 kids, I became aware that not just kids were doing my plays, but teenagers and adults alike. So, a full-length Shakespeare comedic tragedy play was born.

This play follows suit. Edgar Allan Poe, Robert Louis Stevenson, and Washington Irving - were classic authors with classic tales that have survived the test of time. What better way to put them together but in a fun trilogy!

The entire point of this play is to inspire the love of drama and classic stories into the actors and audience. It is your responsibility, as the director, to make sure you create an environment for this to occur. Creativity is key to melodrama. By creating an open, energetic, and engaging environment, two things happen:

1) The artists care more about the end product and making the show memorable and
2) a performance that the audience will never forget!

This being said, if any actor has a creative interpretation they want to try to help tell the story, then let them try it! That's the beauty of rehearsals, it allows us to continue to try new ideas until something sticks and makes us all laugh.

Lastly, any lines you see highlighted in grey throughout the play are ACTUAL text from the original story. So, please don't be TOO creative with these lines! Everything else is fair game!

With these notes, I bid you adieu, break some legs, and most importantly, be creative and have fun!

-Brendan P. Kelso

Setting the Stage

You are doing three 1-act plays in one show, all set between 1720 and 1890. All dark, spooky, and gothic. Knowing that, having a set with a dark vibe and lots of shadows lurking, you'll do great! (especially with Edgar, Hyde, and Headless always hiding out there!) I have always been a minimalist when it comes to sets, as I like the focus to be on the actors. I use black boxes and minimal props for all my shows. I will occasionally do a backdrop if the actors want it. But, this is entirely up to the director and actors on how elaborate and creative they want to be! This part of the art is on you! (also, feel free to send photos! I always love seeing photos of my plays in the wild!)

CAST of CHARACTERS

NARRATOR: our beloved (are they really?) storyteller.

THE LEGEND OF SLEEPY HOLLOW
14 - 20 Actors

ICHABOD CRANE: traveling teacher, always hungry, hopelessly in love with Katrina, not the best looking

[3]**HEADLESS HORSEMAN:** Hessian Soldier who met a grim death (does not have his head!)

BROM VAN BRUNT AKA BROM BONES: the town bully who competes for Katrina's love, good at almost everything. Almost.

[1]**KATRINA VAN TASSEL:** the love interest of Ichabod and Brom

[2]**BALTUS VAN TASSEL:** Katrina's rich daddy

[6]**HANS VAN RIPPER:** Ichabod's current landlord, doesn't like book readers

THE ENSEMBLE

<u>STUDENTS</u>

KID 1: a kid

KID 2: another kid

[1]**KID 3:** and yet another kid

KID 4: the overacting kid

<u>OLD DUTCH WIVES</u>

WIFE 1: not that old

WIFE 2: wears lots of gold

[4]**WIFE 3:** tales foretold

[5]**WIFE 4:** has a cold!

[2,6]<u>HOOLIGANS</u>

HOOLIGAN 1: derelict

HOOLIGAN 2: rascal

HOOLIGAN 3: rogue

HOOLIGAN 4: roughneck

<u>GIRLS</u>

[4]**GIRL 1:** benevolent

[5]**GIRL 2:** gracious

The same actors can play the following parts:

[1]KATRINA and KID 3

[2]BALTUS and a HOOLIGAN

[3]HEADLESS HORSEMAND and ANYONE but ICHABOD

[4]WIFE 3 and GIRL 1

[5]WIFE 4 and GIRL 2

[6]RIPPER and a HOOLIGAN

Anyone can be part of the ensemble at any time

THE STRANGE CASE OF DR. JEKYLL & MR. HYDE
9-14 Actors

UTTERSON: a lawyer who seeks out the truth
[2]**ENFIELD:** friend to Utterson
DR. JEKYLL: good scientist with one REALLY bad idea
MR. HYDE: evil – does whatever he wants
[1]**LANYON:** friend of Utterson and Jekyll
[2]**POOLE:** the butler
[1]**SIR CAREW:** a slow and really old soon-to-be-dead guy
[2]**INSPECTOR NEWCOMEN:** an inspector
[3]**POLICE:** the police
[3]**TRAMPLED GIRL:** a girl that gets trampled
[3]**BRADSHAW:** one of Jekyll's servants
SERVANT 1: another servant
SERVANT 2: and yet... another

The same actors can play the following parts:
[1]CAREW and LANYON
[2]ENFIELD, POOLE, and INSPECTOR
[3]POLICE, GIRL, and BRADSHAW
SERVANTS can be anyone not on stage *(including you, director!)*

NOTE: Both NARRATOR and HYDE are characters that can be improvised throughout the show. NARRATOR is constantly annoying and trying to weave themselves into the story. HYDE takes many liberties, as he does not follow the rules. Be sure to have creative fun with these two characters.

EDGAR ALLAN POE MASHUP
14 - 22 Actors

EDGAR: Edgar Allen Poe, the writer of all the chaos

THE FALL OF THE HOUSE OF USHER

RODRICK USHER: depressing goth guy
[1]**MADELINE USHER:** depressing goth girl

THE MASQUE OF THE RED DEATH
[2]**PRINCE PROSPERO:** a Prince with an ego
RED DEATH: a vicious plague
[4]**PARTY-GOER 1:** likes to party!
[5]**PARTY-GOER 2:** ditto!
BACKSTAGE PEOPLE: they scream then die

THE MURDERS IN THE RUE MORGUE
DUPIN: the first great detective
[4]**MOM:** meets a gruesome death
[5]**DAUGHTER:** meets an even gruesomer death
[3]**CONSTABLE:** yeah, dies, too
[2]**SAILOR:** doesn't die
[8]**ITALIAN:** a person from Italy
[1]**ENGLISH PERSON:** a person from England
[6]**FRENCH PERSON:** a person from France
[7]**GERMAN:** a person from Germany
ORANGUTAN: a hairy, thieving monkey

THE TELL-TALE HEART

[6]**UNRELIABLE NARRATOR:** I wouldn't trust him
[3]**POLICE 1:** a police officer
[8]**POLICE 2:** you guessed it, another police officer

THE RAVEN

SAD NARRATOR: a narrator, but sad and mopey
[7]**RAVEN:** a bird, what else do you think a raven is?

The same actors can play the following parts:

[1]MADELINE and ENGLISH
[2]PRINCE PROSPERO and SAILOR
[3]CONSTABLE and POLICE
[4]MOM and PARTY-GOER
[5]DAUGHTER and PARTY-GOER
[6]FRENCH and UNRELIABLE NARRATOR
[7]GERMAN and RAVEN
[8]ITALIAN and POLICE

Anyone can be part of the ensemble at any time
EVERYONE will be part of the "Backstage people" (including you, director!)

INTRODUCTION

(NARRATOR enters)

NARRATOR: *(to audience)* Hello! Welcome to a night of mystery, madness, and melodrama. Oh, and an exceedingly charming narrator. *(winks at audience)* First, we will gallop to the small, not-so-quaint, village of Sleepy Hollow. Then we will hop over to London, for a personality shift. And finally, we get to dive deep into the perilous poetic pits of… well, you know who.

(raven's sound is heard backstage)

NARRATOR: Poe.

(EDGAR slowly appears from the darkness)

EDGAR: Yes. It's me. Edgar. Allan. POE. Master of the Macabre. The Father of Horror. Gothic fashion trendsetter. And now, apparently, a guest star in a community theater production.

NARRATOR: Edgar! I wasn't expecting you until act three!

EDGAR: Yes, well, someone has to start this show off with proper dread and darkness.

NARRATOR: Yes! That is what I was doing.

EDGAR: Oh, really? Well, boring IS a choice. I mean, if I were opening, the audience would already be weeping.

NARRATOR: That's not very kind, Edgar.

EDGAR: Kind? I don't do kind. Dark. Sinister. Twisted. THAT I have in spades. But kind, no. Now, move over. *(physically moves NARRATOR to side)*

NARRATOR: Hey!

EDGAR: *(to audience)* Once upon an evening dreary. *(points at audience member)* That guy looks awful eerie.

NARRATOR: You can't say that about our audience members!

EDGAR: *(holds hand up to stop NARRATOR)* Prepare yourself for tales so—

(ICHABOD enters)

ICHABOD: Is it my turn yet?! Am I on?!

NARRATOR: No, Ichabod, not yet. *(turns ICHABOD around and offstage)*

EDGAR: As I was saying—

(HYDE enters)

HYDE: Did you say eerie? That's my cue, right? I've got some bottled rage I need to unleash!

NARRATOR: Oh no! Nope! We are not doing this! Hyde, back to your morally grey corner.

(HYDE turns, grumbles, and exits)

EDGAR: Oh! Who was he?! I like him!

NARRATOR: Of course you do. Will you just finish?

EDGAR: Oh, right! Eerie—

RAVEN: *(backstage)* NEVERMORE!

NARRATOR: Not you either, bird!

EDGAR: Is that my raven?!

NARRATOR: What? Oh, yeah. Yes, it is! And she needs you. Go to her!

EDGAR: *(exits)* I'm coming my muse!

NARRATOR: Glad he's finally gone. Shall we try this again? Let's start with our first terrifying tale.

THE LEGEND OF SLEEPY HOLLOW

ACT 1 SCENE 1

NARRATOR: This is a true story, based on fiction, which I heard secondhand from an old farmer, who doesn't exist. So it must be true or urban legend? Confused yet? Good! Hello! My name for this play is Diedrich Knickerbocker, and I'm your narrator for today's creepy adventure. Our story takes place in 1790, in a sequestered glen, known by the name of SLEEPY HOLLOW. Speaking of creepy looking, check out this guy.

(enter ICHABOD whistling and reading a book titled: WITCHCRAFT)

ICHABOD: Oh, I do love these ghost stories!

NARRATOR: Hey sir! Watch where you're going. There have been many terrors of the night down that path.

ICHABOD: Really?

NARRATOR: Yes! There's a drowsy, dreamy influence that seems to hang over the land.

ICHABOD: Sounds fascinating!

NARRATOR: No. Sounds spine-chilling! Why, in the name of all things weird, would you want to go THERE?!

ICHABOD: I am a student of supernatural stories and marvellous beliefs!

NARRATOR: Well then, crazy's waiting for you just down the road!

ICHABOD: Oh goody! *(walks towards "town" offstage)*

NARRATOR: I tried to warn him.

(ICHABOD enters, looks around)

ICHABOD: Well, this town looks like a wonderful place to stay for a while.

(enter WIVES who stop ICHABOD)

WIFE 1: And who might you be?

ICHABOD: My name, dear ladies, is Ichabod Crane. *(he bows)*

WIFE 2: And what do you do?

ICHABOD: I am a schoolmaster.

(WIVES look at each other happily)

WIFE 3: We are looking for a teacher.

ICHABOD: As well as a singing-master. *(starts singing)*

WIFE 4: That's fantastic!

ICHABOD: But, I'm afraid I don't have much money or a place to stay.

WIFE 1: That's ok. If you teach our children, we will gladly house and feed you… a total stranger!

WIFE 2: Yes. We don't believe in stranger danger here and you look smart, I think.

WIFE 3: That's right! We have a lot stranger things to worry about than random people coming through our town!

WIFE 4: Like marvellous tales of ghosts and goblins!

WIFE 1: And haunted fields!

WIFE 2: And haunted brooks!

WIFE 3: And haunted bridges!

WIFE 4: And haunted houses!

ICHABOD: And the supernatural?!

WIVES: Oh, yes!

ICHABOD: Then I'm staying! Now, tell me some stories!

(WIVES start telling a story as they ALL walk offstage; NARRATOR remains)

ACT 1 SCENE 2

NARRATOR: Now for the rest of our characters.

(enter WIVES, gossiping)

NARRATOR: You've met, the old Dutch wives; they run everything.

(WIVES stop)

WIFE 1: We do.

WIFE 2: Who are you calling old, by the way?

NARRATOR: What?! Old? I said… ahhh… cold, yeah! *(smiles)*

WIFE 3: So, the COLD Dutch Wives?

NARRATOR: Ummm...

WIFE 4: Not better.

WIVES: *(in unison)* We'll be watching you!

(WIVES exit)

NARRATOR: That's not freaky at all.

WIVES: *(from backstage)* We heard that!

(enter HOOLIGANS causing trouble with cast members and audience; grab something of NARRATOR'S and play keep away)

NARRATOR: Give me that!

(enter GIRLS; HOOLIGANS do annoying whoop and halloos trying to be cool to the GIRLS)

GIRL 1: You boys are SO immature.

NARRATOR: The village daughters and the town hooligans.

(a loud howl is heard from offstage; everyone hushes)

NARRATOR: And that… *(enter BROM)* is Brom Van Brunt, otherwise known as Brom Bones. Our resident alpha male.

(poses for audience; HOOLIGANS cheer, say things like, "Bones!", "What's up Bonesy!", "Brom, you're the man!"; the GIRLS swoon)

BROM: I'm the town hero.

NARRATOR: *(aside)* Town bully is more like it.

(BROM shoots glare at NARRATOR who ducks behind podium)

BROM: Hey everyone, party at my place!

(poses again, then ALL exit cheering except NARRATOR)

ACT 1 SCENE 3

NARRATOR: *(pokes his head out; looks to audience)* Is he gone? Yes? Good. That guy's a menace!

BROM: *(from backstage)* I heard that!

(enter RIPPER, speaks to NARRATOR; ICHABOD enters opposite)

RIPPER: My, oh my! Who's the exceedingly lank kid?

NARRATOR: That's Ichabod, our protagonist.

RIPPER: Looks like some scarecrow eloped from a cornfield.

NARRATOR: Be nice to him, Hans Van Ripper, we need him for the story... at least for a while.

RIPPER: *(laughs)* Do I havtah?

NARRATOR: Yes.

RIPPER: Fine. But I gonna put him to work. Need to get some meat on those bones. *(ICHABOD approaches)* Seems the old Dutch wives have ya staying at my place.

ICHABOD: Yes sir! You know I…

(RIPPER interrupts)

RIPPER: I hear you're smart?

ICHABOD: Well, I do read a lot of books, sir. There's this one...

(RIPPER interrupts again)

RIPPER: Read books?! You know of any good come of this same "reading"?!

ICHABOD: I… ahh…

RIPPER: *(rambles on)* None! That's what! Books just make you thinks different. Causes trouble. That's why my children no more to school. I watching you, boy. Keep your head down, do your work, and we ain't gonna have no troubles. You hear me?

ICHABOD: Yes, sir.

RIPPER: Good. Now get goin' ta feed my horses.

(ICHABOD exits; RIPPER looks through ICHABOD'S book bag)

RIPPER: Waz this?! Books?! Why that whippersnapper… I'll fix him.

NARRATOR: What are you going to do?

RIPPER: *(grins a devilish smile)* Well, let's just say he shoulda read Fahrenheit 451! *(laughs while grabbing books; starts exiting, yelling offstage)* Boys! We gonna have us a fire! *(exits)*

ACT 1 SCENE 4

(enter ICHABOD and KIDS)

NARRATOR: Anyway, now time for class!

KID 1: Can we learn something fun, now?!

ICHABOD: How about the witch trials?! *(KIDS all cheer)* First, what do you call two witches who live together?

KID 2: Broom-mates! *(KIDS laugh)*

ICHABOD: Ok, one more… why do witches wear name tags?

KID 3: Because it's hard to tell which witch is which!

(KIDS laugh again)

KID 1: Mr. Crane, it's getting dark outside, should we head home soon?

ICHABOD: Oh, jeepers! It is! School hours are over!

KID 2: Why don't you like the dark?

ICHABOD: Because it's scary! Ghosts, goblins, the supernatural, and especially WITCHES come out to play, and they don't play nice!

KID 3: That does sound scary. Let's get out of here!

ICHABOD: Ok, who shall I convoy home today? *(ALL raise hands "Me! Me!")* Hmmm… Which one of you has an older sister?

KID 1: I do!

ICHABOD: Is she a pretty sister?

KID 1: Ummm… I think so.

ICHABOD: Great! Then I'll walk YOU home.

(KIDS bummed, "Aw man… "; ALL exit)

ACT 2 SCENE 1

(enter BROM and HOOLIGANS, ALL laughing; BROM is smiling his glorious, mischievous smile)

NARRATOR: Did you and your gang of roughriders pull another madcap prank on somebody? *(BROM shoves NARRATOR offstage)*

HOOLIGAN 1: That was hilarious!

HOOLIGAN 2: Brom, Master Pranker!

HOOLIGAN 3: Farmer McDonald will never get his cat out of that tree!

HOOLIGAN 4: How did you get him up so high?!

BROM: Well men, it's all about the release and making sure they don't get their pesky claws into you!

(HOOLIGANS all laugh; enter GIRLS following ICHABOD; NARRATOR sneaks back onstage)

ICHABOD: Ladies, first we will warm up our voices. *(they sing a silly song)*

BROM: *(to HOOLIGANS)* Who's the clown?

HOOLIGAN 1: He's the new singing-master of the neighborhood.

BROM: Singing-master?

HOOLIGAN 1: Yes. I think the audience would know him as a choir director.

BROM: Oh... one of those.

HOOLIGAN 2: Yea, and the new pedagogue.

BROM: Peda-what?! Who said you could use fancy words?

HOOLIGAN 2: Sorry. It means teacher.

HOOLIGAN 3: He teaches my sister. She LOVES how smart he is!

BROM: But look at him, he's a dork.

ICHABOD: Okay, ladies, now let's practice our scales. *(sing some silly scale practice; BROM looks mischievous)*

HOOLIGAN 4: Brom, what are you thinking over there?

BROM: Who me? Nothing. *(continues grin)*

HOOLIGAN 4: Sure… nothing kind.

BROM: Well. That's true. *(flashes mischievous smile)*

NARRATOR: *(to audience)* Life was good, until a being crossed their path that causes more perplexity than ghosts, goblins, and the whole race of witches put together, and that was… a woman.

(enter KATRINA; everything stops, ALL eyes on KATRINA)

BROM: She's so hot!

ICHABOD: Be still my beating heart.

(BROM steps in front of KATRINA)

BROM: Hello Katrina, I mean… gorgeous! *(flashes smile; she quickly dodges BROM and joins GIRLS)*

KATRINA: Hello, girls!

GIRL 1: We are so happy you're here!

GIRL 2: Katrina, this is Ichabod, our teacher.

KATRINA: Hello.

ICHABOD: Umm, ahh, bah… Hi!

KATRINA: You've got a way with words. You're cute.

ICHABOD: Baa…daa… thanks?

BROM: *(to HOOLIGANS)* Cute?!?!?! He's got nothing compared to these beauties! *(kisses his biceps)* I'll show her. *(starts flexing, HOOLIGANS start cheering him on; KATRINA doesn't notice while she sings with ICHABOD)*

NARRATOR: Hey Brom, why don't you just join them and sing?

BROM: *(glares)* Why don't I just turn you into a pretzel?

NARRATOR: Easy there, big guy! I can take a hint.

ICHABOD: Okay ladies, that's all for today. *(GIRLS exit)* Katrina, can I… uh… walk you home?

KATRINA: Of course!

HOOLIGAN 1: Dude, she likes him.

BROM: Shut it! Men, get out of here. I need to "take care of business", if you know what I mean.

(HOOLIGANS exit giving high-fives or some other cool handshakes to BROM and others; ICHABOD proceeds to "walk" KATRINA around stage while BROM tries to physically intimidate ICHABOD, flexing, tripping, punching, shoving, while none of his tactics work; ICHABOD awkwardly evades them all over the next few lines)

ICHABOD: Which way to your house?

KATRINA: This way. *(BROM tries something dastardly)*

ICHABOD: Oh, look at that old barn!

KATRINA: It's scary at night!

ICHABOD: I like scary. I hear ghosts and apparitions are around here.

KATRINA: Oh, they are!

(BROM tries something mischievous; bird sounds from offstage)

ICHABOD: Listen to that beautiful bird! It's as beautiful as you.

KATRINA: Awwww.

BROM: *(to audience)* Aw, puke! Who says this corny stuff?!

NARRATOR: Maybe you should try saying something nice?

BROM: *(glares at NARRATOR)* Ummm... alright, I'll try. Hey Katrina.

KATRINA: Yes, Brom.

BROM: Ahhh... you smell nice... like chicken pot pie!

(KATRINA, ICHABOD, and NARRATOR pause for a moment then laugh hysterically at BROM; KATRINA and ICHABOD exit)

BROM: *(to NARRATOR)* What are you laughing at?

NARRATOR: You!

(BROM raises fist at NARRATOR who runs offstage screaming; BROM looks at audience member)

BROM: What are YOU looking at?! *(interacts briefly with audience member, then exits)*

ACT 2 SCENE 2

(enter KATRINA and ICHABOD; NARRATOR enters opposite)

ICHABOD: *(to NARRATOR)* She is exquisitely beautiful. Am I right?

NARRATOR: Yes, she is rosy-cheeked, but she's a little of a coquette.

ICHABOD: A flirt?! No way!

NARRATOR: Way.

ICHABOD: I think she likes me. A girl likes ME! Maybe she could be the one!

NARRATOR: I profess not to know how women's hearts are wooed and won. To me they have always been matters of riddle and admiration.

ICHABOD: Very poetic.

NARRATOR: Thank you. That's why I'm the narrator.

KATRINA: This is my home.

ICHABOD: Wow! This is a mansion!

KATRINA: Yes. Daddy has lots of money. Everything is bursting forth with the treasures of the farm.

ICHABOD: Money? Lots of it?

KATRINA: Yes. Daddy's VERY rich.

ICHABOD: *(to audience)* Okay, confirmed! She IS the one! I need to marry that money! I mean... girl! Yeah, that's what I meant!

(enter BALTUS)

BALTUS: My dear, Katrina.

KATRINA: Daddy! *(they hug)*

BALTUS: Who's this… unique looking fella?

KATRINA: He's the new schoolmaster and my singing teacher.

ICHABOD: Sir, very nice to meet you. Your money is very nice.

BALTUS: Money?

ICHABOD: Money? I meant your daughter. *(grins)*

BALTUS: Okay…

KATRINA: Hey Ichy, Daddy's having a merry-making tomorrow night, you know, a big party. Can you come?

ICHABOD: Can I come?! Does a witch ride a broom?! By gosh, I would love to!

BALTUS: In the meanwhile, would you like to come in for something to eat?

ICHABOD: Golly gee! That would be wonderful! I'm always hungry! Maybe for a sleek side of bacon, or a relishing ham, or maybe even a necklace of savory sausages! Mmm…mmm…mmmm. I've got the dilating powers of an anaconda.

(ICHABOD leads the way as BALTUS and KATRINA give strange looks to each other and follow)

ACT 2 SCENE 3

(BROM and HOOLIGANS enter looking mischievous)

BROM: Boys, ready to have some "ghosts" visit our schoolmaster?

(HOOLIGANS cheer and toss books around stage; laughing, they exit; BROM pauses and poses for audience, then slowly glares at NARRATOR)

BROM: You say one word. *(punches fist into his opposite hand)* and you… *(looks at previous taunted audience member)* Same. *(does one more flex for audience, exits; pause, then ICHABOD and KIDS enter; BROM peeks on stage opposite)*

KID 1: What happened here!?

KID 2: It's a mess!

ICHABOD: Oh, my golly! *(freaking out; BROM giggles)* Do you know what this is?! It's witches! All the witches in the country held their meetings here!!!

KID 3: You're joking!

ICHABOD: Does this look like a face that's joking?! You know what we need to do?

KID 4: What?

ICHABOD: Start a fire! That will exercise the spirit of the witches!

(KIDS make as if they are starting a fire)

KID 1: Oh no! The chimney is stopped up.

KID 2: We're being smoked out.

ICHABOD: Aghhh!!! They're out to get us! Everyone run!

(ICHABOD runs offstage leaving KIDS by themselves; KIDS shrug then exit running)

KIDS: No school!

(BROM enters laughing maniacally)

BROM: That'll teach him! *(exits glaring at NARRATOR)*

ACT 3 SCENE 1

(enter ICHABOD, BALTUS, BROM, KATRINA, WIVES; various party-goers eating yummys; ICHABOD continuously scarfs food)

ICHABOD: This food is amazing!

KATRINA: *(to ICHABOD)* Do you dance?

ICHABOD: Ummmm… Ahhh…

BROM: *(to BALTUS)* I bet he dances like a fool!

BALTUS: Like a wild, windmilling, scarecrow!

ICHABOD: Will you be my partner in the dance?

KATRINA: Of course! *(ICHABOD does awesome dance moves with KATRINA)* Wow! You're amazing!

BROM: Darn! He's actually good!

(ALL stand around and watch; BROM sits in the corner and broods)

NARRATOR: He is downright animated and joyous. Brom, on the other hand, is pathetic and jealous.

BROM: And can still hear you. *(scowls at NARRATOR)*

NARRATOR: Whoops! Sorry!

(dancing continues, getting audience involved, by clapping or some other means)

ICHABOD: Okay. Need to fuel this dancing machine with food and drink!

(ICHABOD starts consuming food and overhears the WIVES talking)

WIFE 1: Let's dole out some wild and wonderful legends.

WIFE 2: Yes! Like dismal tales of funeral trains!

(ICHABOD joins them; ALL others listen in)

WIFE 3: Oh, what about the mourning cries heard about the great tree?!

WIFE 4: Oh! That's where unfortunate Major André was taken.

WIFE 1: Yes!

WIFE 2: I've heard the woman in white shriek!

WIVES: NOOOO!!!

WIFE 2: Yes!

ICHABOD: What?!

WIFE 3: A woman perished at Raven Rock.

WIFE 4: And on winter nights before a storm, you can hear her shriek!

ICHABOD: No!

WIVES: Yes!

(thunder rumbles from offstage)

ICHABOD: What was that?!

BALTUS: Must be a spooky storm coming!

(ICHABOD looks scared)

BROM: Ladies, why don't you tell our wonderful teacher here about the REAL legend?

(WIVES look at each other, unsure)

ICHABOD: What?!

BROM: Well, if you won't, then I will!

(WIVES hold their hands up in unison)

WIFE 1: No! You will not do the story justice.

WIFE 2: We will tell you.

ICHABOD: Tell me what?!

(pause; WIVES get up and prepare to reenact story)

BROM: Oh, come on ladies! It's the...

(BROM is hushed by one of the WIVES)

WIFE 3: It's the Legend of Sleepy Hollow.

WIFE 4: The legend of... *(turns to audience)* the Headless Horseman! *(everyone gasps)*

ICHABOD: Headless?!

BROM: Headless!

WIFE 1: Shhh... this is our tale.

WIFE 2: Yes! He is known as the Galloping Hessian of the Hollow.

ICHABOD: Creepy! I love it!

WIFE 3: His ghost rides in nightly quest of his head.

ICHABOD: His head?!

BROM: His head!!!

(WIVES shush BROM)

WIFE 4: His head had been carried away by a cannon-ball!

ICHABOD: What?!

BROM: And the legend says, if he can't find his head, he'll gladly use SOMEONE ELSE'S!!!

(ICHABOD is visibly scared)

WIFE 1: But, don't worry. All you have to do is make it to the old church bridge.

WIFE 2: Yes! Rumor is, he'll vanish in a flash of fire!

WIFE 3: And you'll be safe.

ICHABOD: Hmmm, it's almost as if you're telling me some future important plot point.

WIFE 4: Hmmm, maybe.

BALTUS: It sure is dark and spooky outside. Ok, everyone be-headed home! Goodnight!

(ALL quickly exit except ICHABOD who looks around a little freaked out)

ICHABOD: Ummm… Katrina?

KATRINA: *(pokes her head onstage)* Yes?

ICHABOD: Can I have a word?

KATRINA: Sure Ichy, what's up? *(enters)*

(ICHABOD gets down on one knee)

ICHABOD: Katrina, will you marry me?

KATRINA: Oh, Ichy! How wonderful! No. Goodnight!

(KATRINA quickly exits leaving ICHABOD stunned)

NARRATOR: Ouch!

ICHABOD: Okay then… time to go home. Now, where's Gunpowder?

NARRATOR: *(gets horse)* You do realize this old horse has one eye without its pupil!

(NARRATOR hands ICHABOD Gunpowder)

ICHABOD: Whatever.

(ICHABOD starts the slow horse-walk of shame home, hearing nocturnal forest sounds)

NARRATOR: Only two miles, through the dark, deserted forest. You got this.

ICHABOD: But, did you hear all those ghost stories?

NARRATOR: Sure did. Have a fun ride home!

(owl hoots, scares ICHABOD)

ICHABOD: Wh…what was that?!

NARRATOR: Just a barn owl.

ICHABOD: Oh, yeah, right. I knew that.

NARRATOR: You know, for a guy who loves ghost stories, you sure get freaked out easily.

(shriek is heard; ICHABOD screams and is visibly scared)

NARRATOR: Now, that was probably just the wind whistling through the old locust-trees or maybe the shriek of the woman in white. Who knows? I'd get a move on if I were you.

(ICHABOD starts galloping faster)

ICHABOD: Let's go Gunpowder.

NARRATOR: *(to audience)* All the stories of ghosts and goblins in the afternoon now came crowding upon his recollection.

(thunder is heard; ICHABOD stops, looking around nervously)

ICHABOD: It's the enormous tulip tree!

NARRATOR: Ah, yes, Major André's tree.

(an eerie wail is heard)

ICHABOD: Ahhh… it's him! *(tries to gallop faster)* Come on, you old mule!

NARRATOR: THAT was definitely mourning cries and wailings! You're on your own! I'm out of here! *(exits)*

ICHABOD: You know it's a scary story when the narrator doesn't even stay around.

(as ICHABOD slowly wanders around the stage, other various creepy forest sounds are heard; meanwhile, the HEADLESS HORSEMAN slowly appears on his horse holding a pumpkin)

HEADLESS: *(to audience)* Time for some, hide-and-go-shriek! *(HEADLESS sneaks up behind ICHABOD)* Boo!

ICHABOD: Ahhhhhhhhhhh…. *(frantically runs everywhere to get away, including through the audience; HEADLESS chases and taunts the entire time)*

ICHABOD: Ahhhhhhhhh!!!!! If I can but reach that bridge, I am safe!

(more dodging and weaving around HORSEMAN)

ICHABOD: Come on Gunpowder! You are literally killing me! Let's lose this strange midnight companion! Look, there's the old bridge!

(ICHABOD runs offstage; HEADLESS throws head after him)

HEADLESS: You like my pumpkin?! It's organic so it's SUPER-natural!!!

(HEADLESS exits laughing and howling)

ACT 3 SCENE 2

(enter NARRATOR)

NARRATOR: Hans Van Ripper was quite upset the following morning. Gunpowder, the black steed, was found without his saddle.

(enter RIPPER)

RIPPER: Ichabod! My horse is missing its saddle! Ichabod?! ICHABOD??? Hmmm… I know what'll work… *(hollers offstage)* BREAKFAST!

NARRATOR: But even food could not lure him out… *(RIPPER looks around, shrugs, exits)* Meanwhile, his students assembled at the schoolhouse.

(enter KIDS, goofing off while waiting)

KID 1: I wonder where Mr. Crane is?

KID 2: Probably sleeping in the woods like Old Rip VanWinkle!

(KIDS laugh)

KID 3: You know, if the teacher's not here within 10 minutes, we're free to go! It's the law!

KID 4: Awesome! Oh look, it's 10 minutes now! Later gators! I'm going down to the banks of the brook!

(KID 4 exits, ALL follow cheering; enter RIPPER)

NARRATOR: Dinner had come and gone, and even Hans Van Ripper now began to feel some uneasiness about the fate of poor Ichabod, and, of course, his saddle.

RIPPER: *(yells offstage)* Boys! Let's go find my saddle!

NARRATOR: And… Ichabod?

RIPPER: Oh yeah, and that weird fella, too. *(exits)*

ACT 3 SCENE 3

(enter ALL but ICHABOD and KIDS; everyone is "searching" around stage; RIPPER is holding a saddle)

NARRATOR: Any luck?

RIPPER: Yep! Found my saddle!

NARRATOR: I meant finding Ichabod.

RIPPER: Oh. Dunno.

BALTUS: We've searched everywhere, and no sign of Ichabod.

WIFE 1: I bet he was eaten by a goblin!

WIVES: No!

WIFE 1: Yes!

BALTUS: I think he was just scared from all the ghost stories, yesterday!

(ALL nod in agreement)

KATRINA: I think his heart was broken.

NARRATOR: Why?

KATRINA: Because. I turned down his proposal for marriage.

(ALL gasp)

BROM: It's none of that.

(BROM pauses for effect, down-center, all eyes on him)

NARRATOR: Then tell us, what?!?!

BROM: Last night...

ALL: Yeah...

BROM: As I was riding home...

ALL: Yeah...

BROM: I heard...

ALL: Yeah...

BROM: The Headless Horseman!

(ALL gasp)

NARRATOR: So?

BROM: SO?! Isn't it obvious?! Ichabod has been carried off by the Galloping Hessian!!!

NARRATOR: What? That's silly. That's just a made-up story by some old Dutch settlers.

RIPPER: You talking 'bout us?

NARRATOR: What?! No! *(to audience)* Maybe?

BROM: Is it?! Then, how do you explain... THIS!

(KIDS enter with Ichabod's hat and a broken pumpkin)

KID 1: We found Mr. Crane's hat, trampled down by the church bridge.

KID 2: Next to a shattered pumpkin!

KID 3: The Headless Horseman got him!

KID 4: Aghhhhhhh!!!!

(ALL stare at KID 4)

KID 4: What? I was adding dramatic effect.

NARRATOR: Wow. Ok. Well then...

BROM: Well then, I think we've heard the last of that old schoolmaster!

KID 1: We didn't like school anyway.

KID 2: Let's go back down to the creek!

KIDS: Yay!

(ALL exit)

NARRATOR: And THAT was the last this town ever heard of poor Ichabod Crane.

EPILOGUE

(enter WIVES; KATRINA and BROM enter holding hands)

NARRATOR: *(to audience)* It's been years, and the body of the schoolmaster has never been discovered. No one knows what happened to poor Ichabod Crane.

WIFE 1: Oh, we do!

WIFE 2: Did you not listen to the last scene? The headless horseman took his body and carried him away!

NARRATOR: Well, I heard Ichabod Crane was still alive, in New York, and turned politician.

WIFE 3: Nope. Nope. Nope. The old school house is haunted by the ghost of the pedagogue.

WIFE 4: It's true! I have heard his faint singing on still summer evenings.

NARRATOR: Really? Well, it wouldn't surprise me around these parts, and it is well known that the old country wives are the best judges of these matters. Brom, you're rather quiet over there, what do you think?

BROM: Who me? *(shows an impish grin to the audience)* No idea! But, what I do know, is that I have her!

KATRINA: And I have him!

(BROM and KATRINA exit laughing maniacally)

NARRATOR: Well, he's not suspicious at all. *(to audience)* So that ends our tale: The Legend of Sleepy Hollow. Honestly, between you and me, I don't believe one-half of it myself. But… what do you think? Ghost, politician, or victim of the Headless Horseman?!

(ALL exit but NARRATOR)

FIRST TRANSITION

NARRATOR: As you think on that, let's skip ahead about 90 years, and travel to the foggy streets of London, shall we? We are going from a story where a man loses his head to where a man loses his soul.

EDGAR: *(appears from the shadows again)* And then mine, where they lose their minds…

NARRATOR: Not you again! Third act, remember? Don't you have a bird to find?

EDGAR: I did. She's rehearsing now.

RAVEN: *(backstage)* NEVERMORE!

EDGAR: *(yells backstage)* More ominous!!!

(HYDE enters)

HYDE: You want ominous?!

NARRATOR: No, no, no! Not again.

EDGAR: *(to HYDE)* Please, without me, there is no "Hyde".

HYDE: I'm chemistry, not poetry… Poe.

EDGAR: You're just my Tell-Tale Heart with a Victorian haircut.

NARRATOR: Hyde! You're on in two. Now hide backstage!

HYDE: Fine! But, we're not done here! *(exits)*

NARRATOR: *(to EDGAR)* You, too! Go train that bird of yours.

EDGAR: *(sinister smirk)* You know, I'm beginning not to like you.

NARRATOR: Whatever. As if you like anybody. *(pushes EDGAR offstage, addresses audience)* Finally! Our next tale is Dr. Jekyll and Mr. Hyde. The debate about man's duality of good and evil. Oh, and good news for you all, I get to narrater this story as well!

THE STRANGE CASE OF DR. JEKYLL & MR. HYDE

ACT 1 SCENE 1

Story of the Door

(UTTERSON and ENFIELD enter)

UTTERSON: Ummm… excuse me… Robert Louis Stevenson clearly made me the narrator.

NARRATOR: *(mocking UTTERSON)* Ummm… you're excused and ya boring! And, you're a lawyer, like anyone's going to trust you!

UTTERSON: Rude!

NARRATOR: Anywhoo… Welcome to London in the 1800s. As I was saying, it's a fine, sunny, Sunday…

ENFIELD: Well, hello Mr. Utterson.

UTTERSON: Hello to you, Mr. Enfield.

ENFIELD: Want to hear a fun tale?!

UTTERSON: No.

ENFIELD: Ugh! So boring!

NARRATOR: Like I said…

(UTTERSON glares at Narrator)

ENFIELD: Your face is never lighted by a smile. You see that door right there? It has a very odd story.

UTTERSON: You're going to tell me anyway, aren't you?

ENFIELD: We have an audience, have we not?

UTTERSON: Very well, proceed.

ENFIELD: It was 3 am on a winter's morning, and the streets were deserted.

NARRATOR: Oh! Filled with cakes and scrumptious treats?!

ENFIELD: Noooo. One 's', not two. Nobody's outside. Sheesh.

NARRATOR: Ohhh… would have been better with treats!

ENFIELD: Anyway, I saw this man and a young lady walking towards each other. This man ran into her, trampled calmly over and left her screaming on the ground. And then, he started to hobble away!!! Watch! *(HYDE and GIRL enter and recreate scene)*

(NARRATOR grabs HYDE as he tries to exit)

NARRATOR: No you don't, get back here! *(HYDE stands there very calm)*

HYDE: Listen, I'll pay you a LOT of money if we can just make this… go away.

NARRATOR: OK!

HYDE: *(hisses at NARRATOR who hides)* Not you! Her!

GIRL: Hmmm… ok!

ENFIELD: So, this weird looking guy goes in THAT strange door and comes back with 10 pounds of gold and a check for 90 pounds!

NARRATOR: 90 pounds of scrumptious treats?!

ENFIELD: Pounds is what we call money.

NARRATOR: Ohhh… sorry.

GIRL: Thanks!

(GIRL hobbles offstage; HYDE exits)

UTTERSON: Wow, that IS interesting.

ENFIELD: No… what's REALLY interesting is he came out with another man's check. Signed by the very well-known Dr. Jekyll!!!

UTTERSON: Dr. HENRY Jekyll?!

ENFIELD: The very one! It MUST be blackmail. I've watched the door and the only one who goes in and out is that villainous man!

UTTERSON: Do you know his name?

ENFIELD: Goes by the name of Hyde. And there's something wrong with his appearance, something displeasing, something downright detestable.

UTTERSON: Interesting.

ENFIELD: Very! Oh, it's getting late, must leave! Cheerio!

UTTERSON: Bye.

(ENFIELD exits)

ACT 1 SCENE 2

Search for Mr. Hyde

UTTERSON: *(to audience)* Very strange… you see, Dr. Jekyll's a client of mine. And his will says that all of his belongings go to Edward Hyde. Yes! The same Hyde. But, that's not the strange part; no… it's how it's worded, "Dr. Jekyll's disappearance or unexplained absence."

NARRATOR: *(to audience)* With this thought, Utterson decided he would stalk the mysterious man!

UTTERSON: If he be Mr. Hyde . . . I shall be Mr. Seek.

(enter LANYON)

NARRATOR: Dr. Lanyon. An old college friend of Utterson and Jekyll.

UTTERSON: Hello, Lanyon.

LANYON: Hello, Utterson! *(they shake hands)* What brings you around here?

UTTERSON: You and I must be the two oldest friends that Jekyll has?

LANYON: I suppose we are. And what of that? I see little of him now.

UTTERSON: Did you ever come across a protégé of his, one Hyde?

LANYON: Hyde? No. Never heard of him. As for Jekyll, he began to go wrong, wrong in the mind. He kept talking nonsense, unscientific balderdash!

UTTERSON: Well, that is very interesting. Thank you, Lanyon.

LANYON: Hmmm… Perhaps I should stop by and say hi to our old friend. Goodbye, Utterson.

(LANYON exits)

UTTERSON: Goodbye. *(looks around)* Now, where is Hyde hiding?

NARRATOR: And they meet…

(enter HYDE)

UTTERSON: Mr. Hyde, I think?

HYDE: *(taken aback, and hisses)* That is my name. What's your issue?

UTTERSON: I am looking for Dr. Jekyll.

HYDE: He's not here.

UTTERSON: Let me see your face, sir.

HYDE: Why? Tell me how you know of me?

UTTERSON: We have common friends.

HYDE: *(snarls)* LIAR!!! *(suddenly exits)*

UTTERSON: Rude! *(to audience)* Did you see that murderous mixture of timidity and boldness? He seemed hardly human. I need to see Dr. Jekyll! *(walks across stage; knocks on door; POOLE enters)* Hello Poole, is Dr. Jekyll in?

POOLE: I'm sorry sir, but Dr. Jekyll is out.

UTTERSON: What can you tell me about Edward Hyde? I see he has a key to the back room.

POOLE: Ah, yes. Mr. Hyde has a key. We have orders to obey him.

UTTERSON: Thank you.

POOLE: Good day, sir. *(POOLE exits)*

UTTERSON: *(to audience)* That evil Hyde definitely has secrets of his own, black secrets. What has Jekyll gotten himself into?

(UTTERSON exits)

ACT 1 SCENE 3

Dr. Jekyll Was Quite at Ease

(enter DR. JEKYLL and UTTERSON)

NARRATOR: Soon, Dr. Jekyll hosted a party, and Utterson was determined to question his dear old friend...

JEKYLL: Thank you for coming to my pleasant dinner party. I always enjoy your company, Mr. Utterson.

UTTERSON: I've been wanting to speak to you, Jekyll. You know that will of yours?

JEKYLL: You are unfortunate in such a client. I never saw a man so distressed as you were by my will.

UTTERSON: You know I never approved of it.

JEKYLL: Yes, you have told me so. Again and again.

UTTERSON: Well, I tell you again. Because I have learned more of young Hyde. What I heard was abominable.

JEKYLL: *(surprised)* Listen to me. DROP THIS. You do not understand my position.

UTTERSON: Jekyll, I am a man to be trusted. I am a lawyer. *(NARRATOR starts laughing; to NARRATOR)* Don't laugh.

NARRATOR: Sorry, you said "trust" and "lawyer" in the same sentence. And...yeah... My bad. Go on.

UTTERSON: *(to JEKYLL)* Tell me in confidence and I can get you out of it.

JEKYLL: I can be rid of Mr. Hyde when I choose. This is a private matter, and I beg of you to let it sleep.

UTTERSON: Fine, I will let it go... for now.

JEKYLL: Good. *(JEKYLL and UTTERSON exit)*

ACT 2 SCENE 1

The Carew Murder Case

NARRATOR: One year later, on a quiet and beautiful London night.

(enter HYDE, with cane, who spooks NARRATOR and addresses audience; NARRATOR frantically runs off stage)

HYDE: That guy's rather boring, don't you agree? Let's light my great flame of anger a bit. Meet Carew… an old, OLD guy who is sooooo slow!

(CAREW enters slowly)

CAREW: *(slowly)* Excuse me, can you tell me how to get to the station?

HYDE: Ahhh… no.

CAREW: You see I'm a bit lost and can't quite read this map. Here, let me show you. *(pulls out map but can't seem to do it fast enough for HYDE)*

HYDE: *(impatient, rolls eyes, checks watch, finally opens map)* I must go! What part of 'no' don't you understand?

CAREW: Here… the station here… *(talking to self)* or is it here? Maybe here?

HYDE: *(getting very angry and agitated)* Old man, you are bothering me! Now move out of my way or die!

CAREW: Here it is! *(shoves map towards HYDE)*

HYDE: No… HERE it is! *(hits CAREW with cane)*

CAREW: Ouch!

HYDE: You're annoying and need to die! *(hits CAREW again and drops cane)*

CAREW: What?! Noooooo…..

(CAREW slowly dies; HYDE runs off very crazy and agitated; INSPECTOR and POLICE enter and examine CAREW'S body; NARRATOR pokes head out and slowly comes back onstage)

NARRATOR: *(to audience)* It's Scotland Yard! I'm safe now!

INSPECTOR: Any identification?

POLICE: No sir, Inspector Newcomen. But, we did find this note addressed to Mr. Utterson.

INSPECTOR: Great. Go get him.

POLICE: Yes sir!

(POLICE exits; NARRATOR examines body and INSPECTOR shoos him away; POLICE returns with UTTERSON; POLICE talks with NARRATOR aside)

INSPECTOR: Mr. Utterson, do you know who this is?

UTTERSON: Unfortunately, I do. It's the politician, Sir Danvers Carew.

INSPECTOR: Oh, that's bad. Here is the murder weapon. *(shows cane)* Have you seen it before?

UTTERSON: Oh my, yes I have. I gave this to Dr. Jekyll many years ago. I know EXACTLY who the murderer is. Mr. Hyde is your murderer.

INSPECTOR: Well then, let's try to find him!

POLICE: Ah, sir. Apparently, no one has seen this guy more than twice. But that random character over there, who refers to himself as 'Narrator', says he's ugly and has a haunting sense of unexpressed deformity.

INSPECTOR: Eww. Well then, let's just leave this to Mr. Utterson to figure out! Good luck! *(INSPECTOR and POLICE exit)*

UTTERSON: *(to audience)* Hmmm… time to talk with Jekyll.

NARRATOR: Yes, let's!

UTTERSON: Ummm… not "let's". You. Over there. *(points to corner)*

NARRATOR: Right. Sorry. It's just getting so exciting, being an investigator, catching a murderer. So much suspense!

UTTERSON: OVER. THERE.

NARRATOR: Got it! *(slowly moves over to corner while mocking UTTERSON to audience)*

ACT 2 SCENE 2

Incident of the Letter

(HYDE enters and sits with an audience member)

HYDE: This will be good, I've got them all fooled!

NARRATOR: Hey!

HYDE: Ah, ahh… Shhh… they can't see me. And, if you say anything, I'll ahh… add you to the body count. Got me?

NARRATOR: See who? I don't see ANYONE except Utterson joining the sick looking Dr. Jekyll.

(enter UTTERSON; DR. JEKYLL is sitting on the opposite side of stage)

UTTERSON: Jekyll, you look awful, deathly sick.

JEKYLL: Yes.

HYDE: *(to audience member)* He does, doesn't he? Ha, hah!

UTTERSON: You have heard the news?

JEKYLL: Yes, I have.

HYDE: *(getting excited)* Here it comes!

UTTERSON: I need to know. You have not been mad enough to hide Hyde, have you? …You?

JEKYLL: Me? Me?! No. No! Listen carefully. HE. IS. GONE. Mark my words, he will never more be heard of. You see… he left this letter. *(hands letter to UTTERSON)*

UTTERSON: It says…

(UTTERSON reading as HYDE jumps up center stage and faces audience)

HYDE: It says, "I'm escaping, bye, bye. Oh, and the doctor is safe. Signed, Edward Hyde." And BOOM! Those fools think I'm gone! Ta-ta! *(HYDE runs offstage laughing evilly)*

NARRATOR: *(to audience)* Strange dude.

HYDE: *(pops up behind NARRATOR, scaring him)* I am, aren't I! *(exits laughing evilly again)*

UTTERSON: Hmmm…

JEKYLL: I have lost confidence in myself. I am the most miserable human.

UTTERSON: Easy there. Get some rest. I'll see myself to the door. Goodnight.

JEKYLL: Goodnight.

(JEKYLL exits; UTTERSON walks to POOLE as he enters)

UTTERSON: Question, who delivered the letter today?

POOLE: There was no delivery today, sir.

UTTERSON: None?

POOLE: Nothing, sir.

UTTERSON: Thank you. *(POOLE exits)* Well, that's strange. How did the letter get here? Did Henry Jekyll forge for a murderer?! *(to audience)* Oooh, this is getting interesting!

NARRATOR: He has no idea!

(UTTERSON exits)

ACT 2 SCENE 3

Incident of Doctor Lanyon

NARRATOR: Good news! It's been four months and we haven't seen hide nor hair of Hyde! Thankfully! Because he was up to all sorts of debauchery! You might say the death of Sir Danvers was more than paid for by the disappearance of Mr. Hyde.

(UTTERSON enters)

UTTERSON: Since then, Dr. Jekyll has regained his health and is entertaining again!

(JEKYLL and LANYON enter and join UTTERSON; NARRATOR joins them; ALL look at NARRATOR and shoo him away)

LANYON: Jekyll, you throw the best parties!

UTTERSON: You really do!

JEKYLL: Thank you. See you again next week?

LANYON & UTTERSON: Absolutely!

(LANYON, UTTERSON, and JEKYLL cheers and exit)

NARRATOR: *(to audience)* The trio were inseparable, until…

(UTTERSON knocks on the door; POOLE enters)

POOLE: Hello, Mr. Utterson. Dr. Jekyll is confined to the house and is seeing no one. Good day.

(POOLE exits)

UTTERSON: Ok, that's weird. I'll try again tomorrow.

(POOLE enters)

POOLE: Tomorrow will not work. And please do not come back the day after that, either. Good day.

UTTERSON: What about…

POOLE: No. Good. Day.

(POOLE exits)

UTTERSON: *(mocks him)* Good day! Hmph! I know! Lanyon.

(LANYON enters looking deathly ill)

LANYON: Hello, Utterson. I don't feel well.

UTTERSON: Or look well. It's almost as if you have a death-warrant written upon your face.

LANYON: I am a doomed man. I have had a shock, and I shall never recover.

UTTERSON: Jekyll is ill, too. Have you seen him?

LANYON: Stop. I am quite done with that person.

UTTERSON: That's rather harsh, don't you think? We are very old friends, we shall not live to make others.

LANYON: I'm good with that. My days are numbered anyway.

(LANYON exits)

UTTERSON: That makes me mad. I need to write Jekyll. *(pulls out paper, writes, hands to NARRATOR to deliver)*

NARRATOR: *(reading)* Dear Jekyll, you're being a meany. Stop it! *(to audience)* Oh, snap! *(delivers offstage; pause, JEKYLL enters and hands letter to UTTERSON, then addresses the audience; UTTERSON acts as if he is reading the letter)*

JEKYLL: Dear Utterson, I received your angry letter. Boo-hoo. Get over it. The quarrel with Lanyon is incurable.

NARRATOR: Ouch!

JEKYLL: Achem… Going forward, my door will be shut even to you.

UTTERSON: What!?

JEKYLL: I must go my own dark way. But I do ask one last favor, and that is to respect my silence. *(JEKYLL exits)*

UTTERSON: This guy is a piece of work.

NARRATOR: Right?

UTTERSON: Shut it!

NARRATOR: Right!

(LANYON enters)

LANYON: I'm dead now. *(hands UTTERSON an envelope)* Here, read this. *(LANYON falls over dead; NARRATOR checks body)*

NARRATOR: Yep. Look at his face. Death by shock!

UTTERSON: *(reads envelope)* PRIVATE: for the hands of Utterson ALONE. *(opens envelope to find another envelope)* "not to be opened till the death or disappearance of Dr. Jekyll." Really?! You two are killing me!

(ALL exit except NARRATOR)

ACT 3 SCENE 1

Incident at the Window

(enter ENFIELD and UTTERSON)

ENFIELD: Thanks for doing these walks with me again, Utterson.

UTTERSON: Well, my other two best friends are basically dead, so I guess you'll do.

ENFIELD: Thanks?

UTTERSON: Hey look, there's the door we started the play with.

ENFIELD: Yeah. I think Mr. Hyde is gone for good.

NARRATOR: Ummm… considering we're still on stage, probably not.

ENFIELD: Good point. Oh look, it's Jekyll!

(JEKYLL appears at the edge of stage)

UTTERSON: Jekyll, I trust you are better!

JEKYLL: Actually, I'm not. I will not last long.

ENFIELD: He's cheery.

UTTERSON: Come on out. Join us.

JEKYLL: I would love to, but I can't. Just seeing you makes me smile.

(JEKYLL smiles; and then suddenly his face and body contort with looks of terror and despair; JEKYLL quickly exits; UTTERSON and ENFIELD are shocked and scared; they slowly walk around stage without talking for a bit)

ENFIELD: *(dazed)* What was…

UTTERSON: I-I… I… don't…

ENFIELD: I'm freaking out, man. *(starts panicking)*

NARRATOR: *(grabs ENFIELD on the shoulders)* HEY! Stop! What are you doing?

ENFIELD: Panicking!

NARRATOR: You don't panic like that. THIS is how you panic!!!

(runs around crazy and screaming, motions for them to panic; ENFIELD and UTTERSON panic the same way as they exit)

NARRATOR: Well, that was fun!

ACT 3 SCENE 2

The Last Night

(UTTERSON, POOLE, BRADSHAW, and SERVANTS enter)

NARRATOR: About a week later, Utterson decided to confront Jekyll.

POOLE: Mr. Utterson, we are so glad you are here.

SERVANT 1: Yay! *(one SERVANT hugs UTTERSON)*

UTTERSON: What?! This is very irregular.

POOLE: They're all afraid.

SERVANT 2: WE'RE SCARED!!! *(starts crying loudly; ALL SERVANTS follow; NARRATOR joins)*

POOLE: Hold your tongue! *(SERVANTS hush)* There's the doctor's office. Listen carefully. *(POOLE knocks on door)* Mr. Utterson, sir, asking to see you.

HYDE: *(from backstage)* Tell him I cannot see anyone.

POOLE: *(to UTTERSON)* See! That's not my master's voice! It's NOT him!!!

SERVANTS: Not him!!!

POOLE: And he has been crying night after night for some sort of medicine.

SERVANTS: Crying!!!

POOLE: He sends me to see chemists at least twice a day and it's never, "the right stuff"!

HYDE: *(from backstage)* No, it's not!!!

POOLE: See!

UTTERSON: Ok, that is odd. But, supposing Dr. Jekyll to have been, well… murdered,

SERVANTS: Murder!!!

UTTERSON: … why would the killer stay here for eight days?

SERVANTS: Eight days!!!

POOLE: *(to SERVANTS)* Shhhh!!!!

SERVANTS: Shhhh!!!!

POOLE: But, I've seen HIM!!!

UTTERSON: WHAT?! Why didn't you lead with THAT?!

POOLE: *(motions to audience)* To build the suspense.

UTTERSON: Oh. Ok. Go on.

POOLE: A few days ago, I came into the large room and saw HIM! He whipped upstairs and cried out like a rat! He was UGLY and more of a dwarf.

UTTERSON: Well then, we are going to break in that door!

POOLE: Now that's talking!

UTTERSON: Poole, before we go in, I need to know, did you recognize this creature?

POOLE: If you mean, was it Mr. Hyde? Why, yes, I think it was!

UTTERSON: Well, that monster scares the bejeebers out of me!

POOLE: Yes! Chills went down my spine like ice. Bradshaw!

(BRADSHAW approaches, scared and nervous)

UTTERSON: Oh, pull yourself together, Bradshaw!

BRADSHAW: Yes, sir. *(still scared)*

UTTERSON: Ok, go stand guard at the backdoor, in case he makes a break for it.

BRADSHAW: Yes, sir.

(BRADSHAW and SERVANTS exit, wailing and moaning; NARRATOR hides behind UTTERSON who shoos him to the side of stage)

UTTERSON: Ok, Poole, let's do this.

(a door moves to center stage; on one side, UTTERSON and POOLE, on the other, HYDE, pacing nervously)

UTTERSON: *(yelling through the door)* Jekyll, I demand to see you.

NARRATOR: He's not answering.

UTTERSON: Really? I didn't notice! *(to door)* I give you fair warning, our suspicions are aroused, and I must and shall see you.

HYDE: Utterson, please, have mercy!

UTTERSON: Ah, that's not Jekyll's voice, it's Hyde's! Down with the door, Poole!

(POOLE starts to break down door)

HYDE: No! No! No!!! Please, No!!!!

(as POOLE breaks down door, HYDE cries out like an animal, leaves an envelope, drinks vial, and dies; UTTERSON and POOLE enter; they see HYDE'S body, twitching)

UTTERSON: We have come too late. He's dead.

POOLE: I don't see Jekyll anywhere, dead or alive. Sir, this envelope is addressed to you. *(UTTERSON opens it and a letter and an envelope fall out)*

UTTERSON: Here is a signed will. And, in place of the name Hyde, it says… me?

POOLE: What does the envelope say?

UTTERSON: "Utterson, read Lanyon's letter before you read this. Your unworthy and unhappy friend, Henry Jekyll."

NARRATOR: Go and read the letters! I've gotta see how this thing ends!

UTTERSON: Very well.

(All exit except NARRATOR)

ACT 3 SCENE 4

Dr. Lanyon's Narrative

NARRATOR: *(to audience)* Are you ready for the big reveal?! I am!!! Exciting!!

(enter UTTERSON)

UTTERSON: *(opens letter)* Alrighty Lanyon, why did you die? *(UTTERSON starts reading; enter LANYON on other side of stage reading over UTTERSON)* I received a registered…

LANYON: …a registered letter from Jekyll that said; get a vial from his laboratory, wait for a man to arrive at my door, and give it to him.

UTTERSON: Did you do it?

LANYON: Keep reading…

UTTERSON: If you don't, I will die! Signed your friend, Jekyll.

LANYON: So, yeah. I did it. *(pulls a bag out)* And at midnight, a strange short man, with his face covered, and clothes much too big for him, knocked on my door… *(there's a knock, HYDE enters, excitedly grabs the bag, and pulls a vial from it)*

HYDE: Do you want to see? Has the greed of curiosity come over you? It shall be done as you decide.

LANYON: Yeah, I want to see this!

HYDE: Very well! *(pulls off hood)*

LANYON: Aghhhhh!!!! Oh my, gosh!!! You're hideous!

HYDE: Lanyon, you remember your vows. You can't tell anyone! Behold!

(HYDE drinks vial, screams, contorts, gasps, and convulses for a short while)

LANYON: Are you done yet?

HYDE: Hey! This is my moment, just wait… I've got one left! *(more gurgling and yelling and is finally replaced by JEKYLL)*

LANYON: Oh my, oh my! Oh my! Oh my! Oh my, gosh! You're Henry Jekyll!!!

JEKYLL: Yep.

(EVERYONE backstage says, "DUN DUN DUUUUNNN")

JEKYLL: Thanks! See ya tomorrow for dinner? Bye!

(JEKYLL exits; LANYON stands there in stunned silence, shocked)

LANYON: Ahhhhh….

UTTERSON: Are you ok?

LANYON: NO! My life was shaken to its roots. Sleep left me. The deadliest terror sat by me at all hours; my days were numbered, and I died.

NARRATOR: Wow, a bit melodramatic, aren't we?

LANYON: Yes. And I leave you with this, that creature was Hyde, the very murderer of Carew! I'm outta here!

(LANYON exits; UTTERSON closes envelope)

NARRATOR: Well, that's a twist!

(UTTERSON and NARRATOR stay on stage)

ACT 3 SCENE 5

Henry Jekyll's Full Statement of the Case

NARRATOR: And now, the very man who caused all the chaos!

(JEKYLL enters)

JEKYLL: So, are you interested in how I died?

UTTERSON: Well, I'm certainly curious.

NARRATOR: ABSOLUTELY!!! *(to audience)* Are you?

JEKYLL: Then, read the letter.

UTTERSON: Great! Here we go!

(UTTERSON starts reading; JEKYLL starts reading over UTTERSON)

UTTERSON: Dear Utterson, this is my… *(fades off)*

JEKYLL: … this is my confession and factual representation of what occurred to Dr. Jekyll and Mr. Hyde.

NARRATOR: *(sitting with the audience)* Oh, goodie!

JEKYLL: I grew up with a lot of money and good schooling. My parents expected a lot from me, so, I had to follow all their rules.

UTTERSON: I know how that feels!

JEKYLL: But, I knew there was something deeper and darker in me, that I had to suppress and not tell anyone.

UTTERSON: Oh, so man's dual nature of good and evil?

JEKYLL: Exactly. With my superb intelligence and science background, I believed that I could separate these two pieces of a person.

NARRATOR: Ohhh… that could be very sinister.

JEKYLL: Yes, so I learned. In time, I created a concoction that allowed these personalities to be split!

UTTERSON: Enter the infamous, Mr. Hyde?

JEKYLL: Yes. Not only did it change my personality, but my physical appearance, too!

(HYDE enters)

HYDE: With looks like these, who needs enemies!

NARRATOR: *(to audience member)* Oh, I do not like him! *(HYDE growls at NARRATOR who hides behind audience member)*

JEKYLL: Suppressed for all these years, with no nurturing, no wonder he was short, ugly, and well… that.

HYDE: Hey! I still have feelings… ha, ha, ha… no I don't! That's why I could go out and just be my evil self.

JEKYLL: I don't have to feel guilty anymore. I slept like a champ! I could now "Hyde" my evil personality.

NARRATOR: Good one!

HYDE: I was evil and wicked with no constraints, and I partied like an animal! *(party howls)*

JEKYLL: *(points at himself)* Good.

HYDE: *(points at himself)* Evil. *(sinister laugh)*

JEKYLL: Till one day I awoke as…

HYDE: Me! That's right, I learned to transform without the solution. Life… uh… finds a way.

JEKYLL: Needless to say, I was suddenly terrified. Well, this occurred again and…

HYDE: again… and again… because, well, Jekyll is boring. Everyone knows it's more fun to play the villain!

JEKYLL: He's not wrong there. That's when I started upping my dosages… but, over time, he kept coming back whenever I slept.

HYDE: Can't keep an evil man down!

JEKYLL: Until I transformed in the middle of the day at Regent's Park. I felt horrid nausea and the most deadly shuddering and BAM…

HYDE: There I was! It had been two months!!! How dare he try to throw me away!!! I am everything he wanted to be but would not talk about.

JEKYLL: That is when I brought Lanyon into the picture, poor chap.

LANYON: *(from offstage)* THANKS A LOT!

JEKYLL: Sorry! Anyway, I tried to end this. But evidently, the original compound had impurities, and those impurities are what made it work. So, I could not replicate it. I was doomed at that point! That was my true hour of death.

HYDE: Apparently, mine too! *(looks at Jekyll)* Wimp. *(dies wildly)*

JEKYLL: I lay down the pen and proceed to seal up my confession, I bring the life of that unhappy Henry Jekyll to an end.

(JEKYLL dies)

UTTERSON: Wow. Duality. Good vs. Evil. Murder. Suspense.

NARRATOR: And the butler didn't even do it! Quite a story, don't you think?!

SECOND TRANSITION

UTTERSON: Yes. Yes it was. Sooo… what do I do now?

NARRATOR: How about you clean up these bodies and get ready for the third act?

UTTERSON: Oh, great idea! Let's go Good and Evil… *(shoos bodies offstage)*

NARRATOR: Well, that was unsettling. What dark thoughts the mind can create. But, before we dive into the depths of pure poetic Poe misery, it's time for some food. I'm going to go backstage and get something to eat. You should, too! See you soon! *(exits)*

(intermission OR continue with play)

EDGAR: Is that gibbering nincompoop finally gone? *(looks around)* Good. I've got some fun ideas to do to him. In the meantime, you get the joy of watching me write.

(EDGAR starts setting up to write, papers organized; enter ORANGUTAN sneaking behind; shushes audience, distracts EDGAR and grabs papers)

EDGAR: Hey! Give me those!

(chaos chase ensues with ORANGUTAN and EDGAR - improvise as you wish; ORANGUTAN runs offstage and EDGAR follows; moment passes; ORANGUTAN runs across stage, stops, has fun with audience; EDGAR enters)

EDGAR: Stop, you literary looter!

(ORANGUTAN sees EDGAR, throws papers in the air, exits howling and acting like an orangutan; EDGAR follows behind, scrambling to pick up papers, then notices audience)

EDGAR: Oh, hello again. Sorry about the mess. A character from one of my stories has escaped and stole all my writings! He's been running amok backstage, releasing all sorts of characters, and causing chaos and havoc. I finally caught up with him, and well, as you can see, it's a mess! Let's see if we can put these stories back together. *(tries to organize paperwork)*

(enter NARRATOR)

NARRATOR: *(to audience)* I can't believe I've come back. *(noticing EDGAR)* Oh, and it's your turn, isn't it?

EDGAR: Yes. And since you are SO good at being a narrator, how about we continue that? Yes?

NARRATOR: *(reluctantly)* Fine.

EDGAR: Good. *(Snaps or claps)*

NARRATOR: *(looks surprised, like magic was just cast upon NARRATOR)* Wait, what just happened?

(EDGAR motions to set; NARRATOR looks around at "the house")

NARRATOR: It's so dreadful and dreary. A mansion of gloom.

(EDGAR watches NARRATOR, smiles to audience)

EDGAR ALLAN POE MASHUP

ACT 1 SCENE 1

EDGAR: *(to audience)* This is one of my favorite stories: The Fall of the House of Usher.

(EDGAR sits back to watch; NARRATOR goes to "door" and knocks; DUPIN opens door)

NARRATOR: *(confused)* Who are you?

DUPIN: Who am I?! I am zee first great fictional detective. Detective Dupin at your service. And you, *(studies intensely)* are not a murderer, but a narrator of zis... zis story.

NARRATOR: So, are you like Sherlock?

DUPIN: Sherlock? No! He iz like me!

NARRATOR: Wait! I know, Hercule Poirot!

DUPIN: Bah! Did you not hear me say 'first'?

NARRATOR: Ooookay, then... what are you doing in this story?

DUPIN: I am here to capture a murderer.

NARRATOR: Well, there was no murder here, just typical creepy, grim Poe stuff.

DUPIN: Is this not zee Rue Morgue?

NARRATOR: No, this is the House of Usher. *(looks around)* At least I thought it was.

DUPIN: Very interesting. I am studying a fantastical case of a mother and a daughter who were brutally murdered.

(MOM and DAUGHTER enter)

MOM: I was killed?

DUPIN: Oui! Hence the term 'brutally murdered'.

(MOM dies)

DAUGHTER: What about me?

DUPIN: Oui, oui. You die too, although very gruesome. You had been thrust up the chimney... upside down.

DAUGHTER: Ewwww.

DUPIN: Oui, ewwww. Now die.

(DAUGHTER falls over dead)

DUPIN: I must figure out who committed zese vicious murders. *(Looks at audience)* It could've been any one of zese. Zey all look veeeery suspicious.

NARRATOR: I am sure they are all fine... well, except maybe... that one. *(points to random audience member)*

DUPIN: *(studies audience member)* Oui, I zee what you mean. We shall keep an eye on zat suspicious looking character! But, we must get going.

NARRATOR: Get going? Who do you think I am?

DUPIN: You?! You are my sidekick!

NARRATOR: Sidekick?

DUPIN: Oui! The Unknown Narrator. Are you ok? You look a bit confused.

NARRATOR: Unknown narrator? What is going on here?

DUPIN: Do not ask me. You should ask him. *(points at EDGAR; MOM and DAUGHTER sit up to watch)*

NARRATOR: You mean the creepy-looking guy, sitting in the shadows, watching us? Who's been bugging me all night long?

DUPIN: Oui! He iz Edgar Allan Poe. He wrote us.

EDGAR: *(shuffling through papers)* Yes, I am. So sorry this is confusing. My stories got all mixed up. But it is very common in many of my stories that I have an unknown narrator who describes everything and is one of the central characters.

NARRATOR: What? I don't even have a name?

EDGAR: No.

NARRATOR: Well, that stinks. Can I at least get a name?

EDGAR: No.

NARRATOR: What? But why? I want a name. I had a name in the first play.

EDGAR: Oh my gosh, fine. What name do you want?

NARRATOR: *(thinks)* Steve!

EDGAR: Steve?! No, no, no! (pauses) Vance… Vance Ripjoy. Yeah, that sounds like a name I would write.

DUPIN: You two are done here. No?

(NARRATOR and EDGAR look at each other and mumble agreement back-and-forth)

DUPIN: Good! Ok, let'z go… Ripjoy. *(NARRATOR smiles and follows)* We need to study zee bodies. *(motions to MOM and DAUGHTER to lie down; enter CONSTABLE, FRENCH PERSON, GERMAN, ITALIAN, ENGLISH PERSON, and PRINCE)*

NARRATOR: Sooo… what happened to her?

DUPIN: She waz grossly overpowered, I'm afraid.

NARRATOR: And… the other was… stuffed up a chimney?

DUPIN: Oui! You listen well.

ENGLISH: We heard two people!

(ALL nod in agreement)

ITALIAN: One was French!

(ALL nod in agreement)

GERMAN: And the other was Italian!

ITALIAN: Italian?! No! Russian!

PRINCE: Russian?! No French!

FRENCH: No! German!

GERMAN: Nein!

(they all argue, then slowly look at EDGAR, who smiles and waves at them; enter RED DEATH who creepily walks across stage; EVERYONE stands to the side, freaked out)

NARRATOR: Whoa! Who's… or what's that thing?!

(RED DEATH stops and looks at NARRATOR)

EDGAR: *(frantically fiddles through papers)* No, no, no!!!

DUPIN: I do not know. *(steps closer, coughs, than backs up)* It iz a giant mystery, mixed with a conundrum, and wrapped in a big, red burrito.

(RED DEATH touches CONSTABLE)

CONSTABLE: Ahhh! I have sharp pains! Wait, I have sudden dizziness! *(CONSTABLE falls over and dies; DUPIN checks CONSTABLE)*

DUPIN: He iz dead.

EDGAR: *(pulls out sheet of paper and re-organizes it)* Ah-hah!!! Backstage you go! *(RED DEATH turns, dejected, and creeps offstage)* Well, that was unfortunate. Poor chap.

PRINCE: Poor chap?! What was that?

EDGAR: That was The Masque of the Red Death. About a fictional plague in the middle ages.

PRINCE: Plague?! I don't want no plague! You got those pages in order? I do NOT want to see that thing again. Everyone, to one of my castellated abbeys, till we are safe!

(PRINCE exits, FRENCH PERSON, GERMAN, ENGLISH PERSON, and ITALIAN follow; MOM, DAUGHTER, and CONSTABLE get up, look around, exits; DUPIN follows)

EDGAR: *(looking over pages)* Ok, I think we are good.

NARRATOR: Great! Now, how do I get to my friend Rodrick?

EDGAR: Let's see *(fiddling through papers)* I think you should go through that door... right there.

NARRATOR: You think?

EDGAR: Meh, what could possibly go wrong?

NARRATOR: *(mocks him)* What could possibly go wrong? Do you think I'm just some character you can simply write off?

EDGAR: After ther grief you've given me today. *(nods)* Yeah, pretty much... Ripjoy.

NARRATOR: Ugh, you are so frustrating! *(exits; pause, screams, re-enters)* What the heck was that?

EDGAR: Let me see. *(looks through papers)* Ohhh, sorry about that. That was a pit.

NARRATOR: A pit of despair, if anything. I couldn't see. It was like... I was suffocating in there, and it was just full of stench. And some weird sounds. What was that?

EDGAR: Yes, the sounds of your last days. Just you. Darkness. Your mind. And rats… lots of enormous rats.

NARRATOR: Rats? That does not sound like a fun end-of-days to me.

EDGAR: Nope, it's not. But don't blame me, blame the Spanish Inquisition. Nobody expects the Spanish Inquisition!

NARRATOR: The Spanish what?

EDGAR: Seriously? *(to audience)* Kids these days. *(to NARRATOR)* Go look it up! And you're lucky you didn't see the pendulum.

NARRATOR: Pendulum? No, no, no. Never mind! Get me back to my story. Where's Rodrick?

EDGAR: *(scribbles on a piece of paper)* Here he is!

(enter RODRICK)

RODRICK: Where have you been?

NARRATOR: Where have I…?! Oy! Where have you been?!!!

RODRICK: Right here. In my house… depressed. I'm so glad you've come.

NARRATOR: I can tell, by your… complete lack of enthusiasm. You do look so very… very sad. Dark, morbid, and sad. *(to audience)* He's so dark he makes Voldemort look like a Care Bear.

RODRICK: I feel my soul is tied to this house.

NARRATOR: Yes, it is cold and damp in here. You really should move out. Or at least open some windows. *(looks around)* Why aren't there any windows in this place? Strange.

RODRICK: But, my sister. My sister, Madeline, is sick.

MADELINE: *(enters)* I am. *(coughs, then dies)*

RODRICK: Oh, shucks, she's dead.

NARRATOR: Wow, that was super quick. *(glances at EDGAR)*

EDGAR: Sorry, short play.

RODRICK: Yes, she was quite ill. Help me take her down to the tomb?

NARRATOR: Ummm… shouldn't we let the doctor take her? Or maybe the nice folks from the morgue?!

RODRICK: What?! No man, they just want to analyze her for science reasons about why our house and family are so deranged. But we're not! Right?!

NARRATOR: Right! *(suspiciously looks at audience)*

RODRICK: Don't look at them, they can't help you.

NARRATOR: What?! Oh look, her cheeks still have a faint blush! Is that normal?

RODRICK: Ummm… sure? I don't know. Do I really look like I'm in the right state of mind to answer that question?

NARRATOR: Well, that is a good point.

(RODRICK and NARRATOR take MADELINE backstage)

EDGAR: *(to audience)* This is complicated. *(he mutters to himself, while shuffling his papers; RED DEATH slowly creeps onstage, sees audience and approaches)*

NARRATOR: *(enters)* Whoa! Hey Edgar, that red burrito is back! Help!

(RED DEATH glares at NARRATOR)

EDGAR: *(starts frantically shuffling papers; he finds the right one, crumples it up, and throws it off stage)* Leave! And don't come back! *(RED DEATH exits)*

NARRATOR: Whew, that was close! Stay focused, will ya?

EDGAR: Yeah, yeah.

NARRATOR: By the way, I just saw a black cat back stage. It looked really creepy. Is there something I should be aware of?

EDGAR: I'd stay away from him. He's a brute-beast, too creepy for this play.

NARRATOR: Sounds like a plan. Oh look, here comes that French Detective again.

(enter DUPIN)

DUPIN: Ah hah! Zere you are! Ve have work to do!

NARRATOR: We do?

DUPIN: Oui, oui! Ve have a suspect!

NARRATOR: We do?! Well then, can't we just arrest him?

DUPIN: Very interesting question. Because it comes with a very interesting answer.

NARRATOR: Huh?

DUPIN: Look here. Wait. Where are my dead bodies?

(enter MOM and DAUGHTER)

MOM: Sorry!

DAUGHTER: The director was giving us notes backstage.

DUPIN: Please ladies… we need bodies. *(motions to floor)*

MOM: Oh, right.

(they lay down and assume dead positions)

DUPIN: *(to NARRATOR)* You see here. *(pointing to MOM'S throat)*

NARRATOR: Yes, the marks.

DUPIN: Look closer! How far zee marks are apart! Oui?

NARRATOR: Oh, my gosh. This is the mark of no human hand! *(compares with his hands)*

DUPIN: Very good!

NARRATOR: Who could have done such a thing?!

DUPIN: Who? No. No... what! Come with me!

(DUPIN exits; NARRATOR stays onstage, motions to MOM and DAUGHTER to exit; enter UNRELIABLE)

UNRELIABLE: Who are you?

NARRATOR: Who am I? Who are you? I've been in this story the entire time.

UNRELIABLE: I know, I've been watching you and that pale blue eye of yours.

NARRATOR: Excuse me? Blue eye?

UNRELIABLE: Yes! The eye of a vulture!

NARRATOR: The eye of a what?

UNRELIABLE: Nothing. Nevermind old man.

NARRATOR: Who are you calling an old man? I'm not old. *(turns to EDGAR)* Who is this?

EDGAR: Oh, yes, some of my stories have UNRELIABLE narrators, just like you, except you can't quite trust what they're telling you.

NARRATOR: That person is nothing like me.

EDGAR: Mmm-hmm… but, believe nothing you hear, and only half that you see. Although, this one is a bit of a mad…

(he is cut off by UNRELIABLE)

UNRELIABLE: Why would you say that I am mad? Observe how calm I am. Could a mad man do what I am about to do?

NARRATOR: What are you about to do?

UNRELIABLE: What? I wasn't talking to you. You just look the other way you vexing, blue-eyed, old man. *(suddenly cheerful)* By the way, wonderful day, isn't it?

NARRATOR: I'm not old! *(to audience)* Crazy, right? *(walks to EDGAR, they fiddle with the pages)*

UNRELIABLE: *(to audience)* Don't give me that look. I am not mad! I am clever, oh, so clever. I decided to take the life of the old man and that blue eye, which continues to fix upon me, tearing into my soul.

EDGAR: So, I fixed the story. You can go now.

UNRELIABLE: *(looks at NARRATOR)* Wait. You're not the old man I'm looking for!

NARRATOR: I told you!

EDGAR: Your old man is backstage.

UNRELIABLE: Very well then. I must bid him, and his eye, a… goodnight! *(exits with a cheesy evil grin)*

NARRATOR: *(to audience)* A real wackadoo, that one!

UNRELIABLE: *(from backstage)* I am not crazy! *(NARRATOR motions to audience with crazy gesture; enter PARTY-GOERS and PRINCE)*

PRINCE: Another great party!

(EVERYONE cheers)

PARTY-GOER 1: Thanks for locking your kingdom and keeping us safe from the red plague!

PARTY-GOER 2: Yay! You rock! You're the best, Prince Prospero!

(EVERYONE backstage runs onstage, screaming, and huddles, scared; RED DEATH slowly enters; EVERYONE freezes; RED DEATH crosses stage)

RED DEATH: I'm baaaaack!

PRINCE: *(steps forward)* Wait! Who invited YOU inside?

NARRATOR: Not again!

PRINCE: You shall not pass!

(RED DEATH touches PRINCE who dies; EVERYONE does a collective scream)

EDGAR: Oh no! Stop Red Death! *(RED DEATH stops as EDGAR quickly shuffles papers, and then suddenly a couple sheets drop to the floor; EVERYONE gasps, freezes, looks at the papers, then RED DEATH; RED DEATH seizes opportunity to touch EVERYONE from backstage - all die; then starts approaching audience)*

EDGAR: *(fixes paper)* There! Go away!

RED DEATH: Do I have to?

(EDGAR points firmly offstage)

RED DEATH: Fine! *(bummed, leaves)*

(enter POLICE 1 & 2)

POLICE 1: So many bodies.

POLICE 2: How do we get them out of here?

POLICE 1: I don't know. How about we just ask?

POLICE 2: ASK THEM? Ask dead people to move?

POLICE 1: Yeah. Hey, all you dead people, can you get off the stage?

(DEAD PEOPLE wake up, acknowledge POLICE, and zombie off stage)

POLICE 2: Well, look at that.

(enter UNRELIABLE who runs into POLICE)

UNRELIABLE: Oh, hello!

POLICE 1: Hello! Do you live here?

UNRELIABLE: Why yes, I do. Can I help you?

POLICE 2: Well, a shriek had been heard by a neighbor.

POLICE 1: Yes, we have suspicion of foul play.

UNRELIABLE: *(aside to audience)* As they should! Because I killed that old man and his eye!

POLICE 2: Excuse me, but what did you just say?

UNRELIABLE: I said… hi?

POLICE 1: Oh. Hello… again.

UNRELIABLE: *(aside to audience)* You see, I'm not nervous. Because, I outsmarted EVERYONE! I buried the body right here. *(points down)* Right. Beneath. Their feet!!! *(does a crazy chuckle)*

POLICE 2: I'm sorry, but are you saying something?

UNRELIABLE: Ummm… yes! Would you like a treat?

POLICE 1: That sounds wonderful!

UNRELIABLE: *(aside to audience)* Ha, ha! I have them fooled! *(slight pause)* Wait! Did you hear that… that… that sound!?

POLICE 2: Did you say you heard something?

UNRELIABLE: No! I heard nothing. Did you hear something? Because I sure didn't hear the thing you think you might have heard.

POLICE 1: Huh? Are you ok?

UNRELIABLE: Who meeeee? I'm fine! *(aside to audience)* I'm not fine! I definitely hear something! The beating of a heart! *(to random audience member)* You hear something, right? No?!

POLICE 2: *(taps UNRELIABLE'S SHOULDER)* Excuse me.

(UNRELIABLE screams in fear)

UNRELIABLE: Ok, OKAY!!!! I did it, I killed the old man! His tell-tale heart gave me away! He's buried right there! *(runs offstage screaming; POLICE give chase)*

(enter NARRATOR)

NARRATOR: What was that about?

EDGAR: Oh, just guilt tearing at his mind.

NARRATOR: Oh, wonderful. Are all your stories this depressing and gruesome?

EDGAR: On the most part, yeah. Except The Pit and the Pendulum, that has a relatively happy ending.

NARRATOR: Oh, the one where the guy's covered in rats and locked up over a giant deathly pit with a enormous axe swinging over him?

EDGAR: Yeah, that's the one!

NARRATOR: Right. No long term mental damage from that!

(RED DEATH peaks onstage, slowly enters; approaches NARRATOR who cowers trying not to get touched, then points at audience)

NARRATOR: Hey, look at all of them. I'm just one person, but there's a whole bunch there for you to… feast upon, or whatever you do. *(RED DEATH sees audience and approaches them slowly)* Hey Eddie, you really might want to take care of this… thing… like now!

EDGAR: I know! *(pulls out pen)* THE END!

(RED DEATH hears the words, realizing it's over, dejected, meanders offstage)

NARRATOR: Finally!

RED DEATH: *(stops)* Don't worry, I will be back as another plague in a few years. *(exits laughing evilly)*

NARRATOR: Right, like some random plague would come by and shut the entire world down! Never happen!

(enter SAD NARRATOR; slowly mopes across stage)

NARRATOR: Who's this morose looking individual?

EDGAR: He's you, just a sad version.

NARRATOR: What?! Oh wait, you mean another unnamed narrator?

EDGAR: Yep!

NARRATOR: You sure did a lot of those.

EDGAR: Easier for the reader to relate.

SAD NARRATOR: Once upon a midnight dreary, while I pondered, weak and weary…

NARRATOR: Ooh, he's poetic.

EDGAR: Yes. Sit back and watch. One of my favorites.

SAD NARRATOR:

While I nodded, nearly napping, suddenly there came a tapping.

As of someone, gently, rapping, rapping at my chamber door.

(a knock is heard)

Tis some visitor tapping at my chamber door—only this and nothing more.

(opens "door"; enter RAVEN sneaking onstage)

Hello? Anyone there? *(looks around)* I am sad for my lost love Lenore.

RAVEN: Nevermore. *(sounding like a bird squawk)*

SAD NARRATOR: What was that? Was that Lenore? *(yells out door)* Lenore!

RAVEN: Nevermore.

SAD NARRATOR: *(looks around)* 'Tis the wind and nothing more!

RAVEN: *(flys forward to be seen, continuously acting like a raven)* NEVERMORE!

SAD NARRATOR: What's this? Tell me what thy lordly name is?

EDGAR: Quoth the Raven…

RAVEN: Nevermore.

SAD NARRATOR: Well, that's a funny name.

RAVEN: Nevermore!

SAD NARRATOR: Okay, okay, would you stop saying that!

RAVEN: NEVERMORE!

SAD NARRATOR: This is getting maddening. Maybe this is to give me respite from thy memories of Lenore.

RAVEN: Nevermore.

NARRATOR: Rather lacking in language, don't you think? That bird is going to drive him bonkers. It's starting to drive me nuts!

EDGAR: Well, he has a choice. Grieve in his melancholy forever, or move on.

NARRATOR: So, go crazy or learn to keep loving life?

EDGAR: Basically, yeah.

SAD NARRATOR: Tell me, bird, will I ever be able to talk to my sainted maiden the Angels named Lenore?

RAVEN: Nevermore.

SAD NARRATOR: Stop!!! Stop saying that!!!

RAVEN: *(pauses, looks at audience, smiles mischievously)* Nevermore.

(SAD NARRATOR screams in madness and runs offstage)

RAVEN: *(flys around stage then looks at audience)* Bye-bye! *(exits)*

EDGAR: Hah! Clever bird! I didn't even write that last part!

NARRATOR: Clever bird? It just drove him to madness.

EDGAR: Eh, it was bound to happen. Oh look, your buddy.

(enter RODRICK)

RODRICK: She's alive. She's alive!!! We have put her living in the tomb!

NARRATOR: What? Who?

RODRICK: Madeline! That's who!!!

NARRATOR: Madeline?

RODRICK: MY SISTER!!!

NARRATOR: The one we buried?!

RODRICK: Yes. I hear it, I have heard strange noises! Long — long — long — many hours, many days, I have heard it!

NARRATOR: And you didn't even think to check?!

RODRICK: Ummm… no. I dared not speak! It's dark and creepy down there.

NARRATOR: *(aside)* Kind of like you.

RODRICK: What?

NARRATOR: Nothing!

RODRICK: *(enter MADELINE slowly walking on stage, looking very dead)* I tell you that she now stands! *(RODRICK falls over)*

NARRATOR: Rodrick! *(checks RODRICK)* Oh, no! Now he's dead!

(cracking noises from the house are heard; MADELINE continues to walk forward)

NARRATOR: The house is suddenly falling apart! I'm out of here! *(runs offstage; RODRICK and MADELINE slowly exit)*

EDGAR: *(yells backstage)* You can come back now!

NARRATOR: *(peaks onstage then reenters)* What happened?

EDGAR: Like we said earlier, their souls were tied to that house. When they died, so did the house. Lucky you got out of there. I haven't been able to kill you yet.

NARRATOR: Kill me yet? Is that part of your goal?

EDGAR: Or drive you mad. You know, my main themes.

NARRATOR: Oh joy.

EDGAR: Don't worry, there's still time for you to become insane, with long intervals of horrible sanity. *(grins at NARRATOR; moment passes as EDGAR and NARRATOR stare at each other in awkward confrontation)*

DUPIN: *(enters)* My good man! There you are! Ve have a crime to solve!

NARRATOR: Oh, right. Of course. What was I thinking?!

DUPIN: I put an ad in zee local newzpaper: missing Ourang-Outang.

NARRATOR: Ourang-Outang?!

DUPIN: Oui! After further analysis, from my keen eye and extensive intelligence, it waz obvious, waz it not?

NARRATOR: Of course! *(shakes head at audience)*

DUPIN: Oui! The strength to thrust the body up zee chimney; zee size of zee grip around her throat; and zee agility to get up to zee second floor and through zee window.

NARRATOR: An Ourang-Outang? That's kind of a stretch, isn't it?

DUPIN: It iz, for simple police mindz. Unless we look at zee evidence with an open mind.

NARRATOR: You have more?

DUPIN: Oui! The unknown hair found. The strength to pull out a clump of the victim's hair. And zee testimony of our witnesses!

NARRATOR: What testimony? They were inconsistent.

DUPIN: OUI! That was the evidence itself! THAT is what WAS consistent!

NARRATOR: *(pauses, looks at DUPIN)* You make absolutely no sense.

DUPIN: Elementary, my dear… Ripjoy… I do not like that name.

NARRATOR: I do not care!

DUPIN: Zee French is positive that the voice was that of an Italian. But is not cognizant of that tongue. The Italian believes it the voice of a Russian, but has never conversed in Russian. The English thinks it the voice of a German, and does not understand German. A Spaniard 'is sure' that it was that of an English, yet he has no knowledge of English.

NARRATOR: Huh?

DUPIN: Sacré bleu! Each spoke as that of a foreigner, from the other's language.

NARRATOR: So, someone from a foreign land?

DUPIN: That no one from Europe could recognize? No. They said the voice was harsh. So, we put all zee evidence together.

NARRATOR: And you come to Ourang-Outang?

(there's a knock at the 'door'; SAILOR enters)

SAILOR: *(nervous)* Hello? Ummm… you found a missing Ourang-Outang?

DUPIN: Oui! He iz safe, nearby. *(NARRATOR has look of disbelief)*

SAILOR: I am willing to pay a reward.

NARRATOR: How the… you got it right!

DUPIN: My reward shall be all the information about the murders in the Rue Morgue!

SAILOR: *(look of shock)* I… ahhh… ok, the Ourang-Outang did it.

NARRATOR: Whaaaat!!!

SAILOR: We landed at Borneo, where I captured the Ourang-Outang. I got him home and kept him safe in my residence in Paris. I was to sell him. Until he broke out. I chased him through the streets. At three o'clock in the morning, the streets were profoundly quiet. He saw lights on in the Rue Morgue, then all chaos broke out! I am ashamed!

DUPIN: Oui! And off to jail you go! *(DUPIN and SAILOR start to exit; ORANGUTAN runs across stage, exits)*

SAILOR: There he is now!

(SAILOR and DUPIN give chase, exit)

NARRATOR: Wow, what a twist for the ending! That was brilliant, Edgar! I take back everything I've said about you!

(EDGAR approaches narrator, center-stage)

EDGAR: Yes... what a twist. And brilliant? Of course! But, not the best twist of the play.

NARRATOR: What do you mean?

EDGAR: I mean... your name is not Vance Ripjoy.

NARRATOR: It's not?

EDGAR: And I... am not Edgar. I am... *(rips off his mustache)* Montresor, from The Cask of Amontillado!

(EVERYONE backstage says, "dun-dun-dun")

NARRATOR: Then that would make me...

EDGAR: FORTUNATO! My dear friend, but really... *(clasps NARRATOR'S shoulder)* my mortal enemy! You have hurt me. You have insulted me. And now... it's time for revenge!

NARRATOR: R-R-Revenge? I don't like the sound of that.

EDGAR: Then, you will not like the sound of this! *(EDGAR shoves NARRATOR offstage)* You are now locked in the catacombs for the next fifty years! *(evil laugh)*

NARRATOR: What?! Nooooo!!! This is a bit dramatic, Edgar!

EDGAR: Yes, well, it is called *melodramatic theatre*!

NARRATOR: Help! Help… heeeeeeelllllllllp…. *(voice fades away)*

EDGAR: In pace requiescat! *(to audience; replaces mustache, starts with a little evil snicker; gathers papers)* Don't worry about him. He's taken an unexpected intermission. PERMANENTLY. He's locked somewhere between the Act III... and the 1700's. *(ORANGUTAN enters quietly)* And, if tonights performance has left you shaken, stirred, or questioning your own dark thoughts; you're welcome! *(ORANGUTAN quietly sneaks up behind EDGAR, shushing audience)* Till we meet again in your dreams... or nightmares, bye-bye! *(ORANGUTAN grabs papers from EDGAR and runs offstage)* Hey! Comeback here you thieving monkey!!! *(exits chasing ORANGUTAN)*

RAVEN: NEVERMORE!

THE END

ABOUT THE AUTHOR

BRENDAN P. KELSO came to writing modified Shakespeare scripts when he was taking time off from work to be at home with his newly born son. "It just grew from there". Within months, he was being asked to offer classes in various locations and acting organizations along the Central Coast of California. Originally employed as an engineer, Brendan never thought about writing. However, his unique personality, humor, and love for engaging kids with The Bard has led him to leave the engineering world and pursue writing as a new adventure in life! He has always believed, "the best way to learn is to have fun!" Brendan makes his home on the Central Coast of California and loves to spend time with his wife and kids.

Sneak Peeks at other Playing With Plays books:

Shakespeare's Hilarious Tragedies (full-length) .... Pg 96

Beofrankula! A Monster Mash-up (full-length) .... Pg 94

Meddling, Manners, and Matrimony (a full-length Jane Austen trilogy) .... Pg 100

A Christmas Carol (1-Act play) .... Pg 102

The Odyssey (1-Act play) .... Pg 104

Shakespeare's Hilarious Tragedies

A play in 4 Acts

Shakespeare's Hilarious Tragedies is the perfect production for programs looking to engage students, teachers, and audiences alike with a fresh, comedic twist on the Bard's greatest works. This full-length play condenses the dramatic intensity of *Julius Caesar, Romeo & Juliet, Macbeth*, and *Hamlet* into a fast-paced, laugh-out-loud experience—complete with a body counter to keep track of all the "tragic" mishaps!

With flexible casting, easy staging, and a script that blends classic literature with modern humor, this play is an exciting way to make Shakespeare fun, accessible, and unforgettable. Whether you're introducing students to the classics or giving seasoned performers a new challenge, Shakespeare's Hilarious Tragedies guarantees an entertaining and educational experience for all.

Dare to take on the tragedies—if you can stop laughing long enough!

Beofrankula!
A Monster Mash-up

A Comical Melodrama in 3 acts
by Brendan P. Kelso, Angela M. Herrick, and Amanda Thayer

Beofrankula!
A Monster Mash-up

A play in 3 Acts

A Monster-Sized Adventure with Laughter!

Beofrankula! A Monster Mash-up is a full-length, fast-paced comedy that breathes new (and undead) life into three legendary classics—*Beowulf, Frankenstein*, and *Dracula*! Packed with humor, thrilling action, and clever segues that tie these monstrous tales together, this play offers a fresh and hilarious take on literature's most famous creatures.

Perfect for schools looking to engage students with classic stories in a fun and accessible way, Beofrankula! features flexible casting, simple staging, and plenty of over-the-top monster mayhem. Whether you're battling Grendel, dodging Frankenstein's experiments, or trying to survive Dracula's charm, this production delivers endless laughs and spooky fun for all ages.

The legends are bigger. The laughs are louder. The monsters are… well, still monsters!

Meddling, Manners, and Matrimony

A Jane Austen Trilogy

A play in 3 Acts

Three Austen Classics, One Hilarious Night!

Looking for a fresh and funny take on Jane Austen? *Meddling, Manners, and Matrimony* presents the beloved stories of *Emma, Sense & Sensibility,* and *Pride & Prejudice* as a hilarious trilogy of fast-paced, one-act plays with playful transitions by Jane herself! This clever adaptation offers a remarkably flexible ensemble cast size, accommodating between 14 and 47 actors!

Imagine bringing these classic tales to life with your own vision, utilizing a common set and minimal props to keep the focus on your talented cast. This play sparks a love for drama and classic storytelling in performers and audiences alike. The script weaves actual Jane Austen text within the comedic dialogue. With short run times of approximately 25 minutes per act, this trilogy provides an accessible and entertaining experience.

Don't miss the opportunity to present these timeless stories with a playful twist! Delight your actors and audience with the charm of Jane Austen with *Meddling, Manners, and Matrimony*!

Sneak peek of

Christmas Carol

(enter GHOST PRESENT wearing a robe and holding a turkey leg and a goblet)

GHOST PRESENT: Wake up, Scrooge! I am the Ghost of Christmas Present. Look upon me!

SCROOGE: I'm looking. Not that impressed. But let's get on with it.

GHOST PRESENT: Touch my robe! *(SCROOGE touches GHOST PRESENT's robe. Pause. They look at each other)* Er…it must be broken. Guess we walk. Come on. *(they begin walking downstage)*

SCROOGE: Where are we going?

GHOST PRESENT: Your employee, Bob Cratchit's house. Oh look, here we are.

(enter BOB, MRS. CRATCHIT, MARTHA CRATCHIT, and TINY TIM, who has a crutch in one hand; they are all holding bowls)

BOB: *(to audience)* Hi, we're the Cratchit family. We are a REALLY happy family!

MRS. CRATCHIT: *(to audience)* Yes, but we're REALLY poor, too. Thanks to HIS boss! *(pointing at BOB)*

MARTHA: *(to audience)* Yeah, as you can see our bowls are empty. *(shows empty bowl)* We practically survive off air.

TINY TIM: *(to audience)* But we're happy!

MRS. CRATCHIT: *(to audience; overly sappy)* Because we have each other.

TINY TIM: And love!

SCROOGE: *(to GHOST PRESENT)* Seriously, are they for real?

GHOST PRESENT: Yep! Adorable, isn't it?

BOB: A merry Christmas to us all.

TINY TIM: God bless us every one!

SCROOGE: Spirit, tell me if Tiny Tim will live.

GHOST PRESENT: *(puts hands to head as if looking into the future)* Ooooo, not so good....I see a vacant seat in the poor chimney corner, and a crutch without an owner. If SOMEBODY doesn't change SOMETHING, the child will die.

SCROOGE: No, no! Say he will be spared.

GHOST PRESENT: Nope, can't do that, sorry. Unless SOMEONE decides to change...hint, hint.

BOB: A Christmas toast to my boss, Mr. Scrooge! The founder of the feast!

MRS. CRATCHIT: *(angrily)* Oh sure, Mr. Scrooge! If he were here I'd give him a piece of my mind to feast upon. What an odious, stingy, hard, unfeeling man!

BOB: Dear, it's Christmas day. He's not THAT bad. *(Pause)* He's just... THAT sad. *(BOB holds up his bowl)* Come on, kids, to Scrooge! He probably needs it more than us!

MARTHA & TINY TIM: *(holding up their bowls)* To Scrooge!

MRS. CRATCHIT: *(muttering)* Thanks for nothing.

BOB: That's not nice.

MARTHA: And we Cratchits are ALWAYS nice. Read the book, Mom.

MRS. CRATCHIT: Sorry.

(the CRATCHIT FAMILY exits)

SCROOGE: She called me odious! Do I really smell that bad?

GHOST PRESENT: Odious doesn't mean you stink. Although in this case you do… According to the dictionary, odious means "unequivocally detestable." I mean, you are a toad sometimes Mr. Scrooge.

SCROOGE: Wow… that's kind of … mean.

Sneak peek of
The Odyssey

CREW 5: Look! Land!

YOUNG ODYSSEUS: Oh! I almost forgot; we can't stop here!

CREW: WHAT?!

YOUNG ODYSSEUS: It is the most dangerous place yet. Keep going!

CREW 5: They're just a bunch of cows, boss.

CREW 3: Maybe they are mutant cows that will eat us.

CREW 4: I'm tired of being eaten. I need to rest.

CREW 2: Me too!

CREW 6: I'm just tired!

CREW 1: Come on, sir. Let us stop.

YOUNG ODYSSEUS: Alright. Alright. But, you MUST promise not to harm a single cow.

CREW: Promise!

ODYSSEUS: *(to audience)* We came ashore and fell fast asleep. But, during the night, Zeus raised a great gale of wind, causing a hurricane.

CREW 1: Looks like we are stuck here.

YOUNG ODYSSEUS: We have lots of food on the ship. Remember, do NOT kill any cows!

CREW: Yes, sir! No cows!ODYSSEUS: The hurricane blew for an entire month…

ALL: A MONTH!?!?

ODYSSEUS: We ran out of food. The days were long. I left my crew to take a nap. *(YOUNG ODYSSEUS exits)*

CREW 2: He naps at the strangest times.

CREW 3: I've never been this hungry in my life.

(COW enters)

COW: Moo.

CREW 4: Look! There's a nice, juicy hamburger. I-I-I mean cow.

COW: Moo?

CREW 5: Let's get it!

COW: Moo!!!

(CREW chases COW offstage, moo sounds from backstage, CREW enters licking their lips carrying "hamburger" supplies)

CREW 4: Now that hit the spot.

YOUNG ODYSSEUS: *(enters; sees hamburger paraphernalia)* Come on! I told you ONE thing. DO NOT eat the cows!

CREW 5: Sorry, boss. But it was only one.

CREW 4: And it was DELICIOUS!

CREW 1: Finally, the wind died down, and we set sail with full bellies!

(CREW rows)

CREW 2: As soon as we were away from the island, a black cloud formed over our ship.

CREW 3: It's Zeus!!!

ZEUS: *(enters)* Helios says you ate Bessie! My favorite bovine! *(stirs up a storm, ALL blow around stage)*

YOUNG ODYSSEUS: Told you not to eat the cows!

ODYSSEUS: *(to audience)* Zeus let fly his thunderbolts, the ship caught on fire, and the crew fell into the sea.

CREW 3: I guess this is it for us.

CREW 5: Nice knowing you!

CREW 4: That burger was worth it!!!

(CREW exits screaming, ZEUS exits happy)

CAST AUTOGRAPHS

www.ingramcontent.com/pod-product-compliance
Lightning Source LLC
Chambersburg PA
CBHW050654160426
43194CB00010B/1930